PREVENTION OF CORRUPTION ACT 1988- SUPREME COURT'S LATEST CASE LAWS

CASE NOTES- FACTS- FINDINGS OF APEX COURT JUDGES & CITATIONS

JAYPRAKASH BANSILAL SOMANI

Made with ♥ on the Notion Press Platform
www.notionpress.com

Dedicated

To

All the Past & Present Judges of the Supreme Court of India.

Salute to their wisdom.

Salute to their interpretation of Law.

Salute to their elaborative judgement writing.

SUPREME COURT OF INDIA

• • •

Contents

Contents

Preface

Dear Learned Advocates of Trial Court, High court and Supreme Court, Corporate and Individuals.

I am very delighted to provide you a book on PREVENTION OF CORRUPTION ACT 1988- SUPREME COURT'S LATEST CASE LAWS

In this book you will get...

1. Name of the Case i. e. Cause title

2. Relevant Sections discussed in the case

3. Hon'ble Judges/Coram of the case

4.Number of PDF Pages in Original Judgement of the case

5. All available Citations of the case

6. Case Note with appeal allowed/ dismissed or disposed off

7. Facts of the case

8. Hon'ble Apex Court's findings, while dismissing/allowing or disposing the appeal

9. Ratio Decidendi if any.

My special thanks to Manupatra, because of their web portal I can compile this book in well manner. I am also thankful to Notion Press to support me to publish & market this book throughout the Country. Thanks to my Juniors, Advocate Colleagues & Insolvency Professional Colleagues to support me in this venture.

Adv. Manoj Kumar Chowdhary & Adv. Shruti Kriti has helped me a lot to compile this book. I hope this book will add some value addition in the wealth of your legal knowledge. Your positive feedbacks will boost me to compile/ write further books & negative feedbacks will improve my skills. Kindly send your valuable feedbacks by email.

Thanks with Regards,

Jayprakash B. Somani

Advocate, Supreme Court of India

Email: jaysomani64@gmail.com

Web Site:www.jayprakashsomani.com

Call: 9322188701, 8459194576

• • •

Acknowledgements

Printed & Published by
Notion Press
No. 8, 3rd Cross Street,
CIT Colony, Mylapore,
Chennai, Tamil Nadu- 600004

• • •

Managed by
Jayprakash Somani Advocates & Solicitors
Law Firm for Supreme Court of India
Delhi Office
B- 851, 1st Floor, Shivaji Marg, New Ashok Nagar, Delhi 110096.
Call: 9322188701, 8459194576
Supreme Court Chamber
312, 3rd Floor, M. C. Setalvad Block, In front of 'D' Gate, Bhagwan Das
Road, Supreme Court of India, New Delhi 110001
Contact: 8459194576, 9811011747
<u>www.jayprakashsomani.com</u>
Download our app to get access to our Free Videos, Free Bare Acts,
Free Study Material in Legal as well as International Business Regime.
Android App Link ;-https://clpandrea.page.link/cmSm
Ios APp Link :-https://apps.apple.com/us/app/classplus/id1324522260
Login with org code ;- (qywzji)
Web Link ;-https://qywzji.courses.store/
Opportunity for Lawyers/ Social Workers to get Supreme Court Law
Firm JSAS's authorised centre at District Level.
Kindly Message or Call to: 9322188701

• • •

Books are available online in India
1. **Notion Press:**<u>https://notionpress.com/author/jayprakash_somani</u>
2. **Amazon:**<u>https://www.amazon.in/s?k=jayprakash+somani</u>
3. **Flipkart:**<u>https://www.flipkart.com/search?q=Jayprakash%20Somani</u>
Books are available online at International Market

4. Amazon International: https://www.amazon.com/s?k=jayprakash+somani

5. Amazon United Kingdom: https://www.amazon.co.uk/s?k=jayprakash+somani

6. E-Books/Kindle edition at National & International Level: https://www.amazon.in/s?k=jaypraksh+somani

• • •

A. Sreenivasa Reddy vs. Rakesh Sharma and Ors. (08.08.2023 – SC) : MANU /SC/ 0842 / 20 23 10 36 /2023

Relative Section:

Banking Regulation Act, 1949 - Section 46A; Code of Criminal Procedure, 1973 (CrPC) - Section 161, Code of Criminal Procedure, 1973 (CrPC) - Section 197, Code of Criminal Procedure, 1973 (CrPC) - Section 197(1), Code of Criminal Procedure, 1973 (CrPC) - Section 203, Code of Criminal Procedure, 1973 (CrPC) - Section 216, Code of Criminal Procedure, 1973 (CrPC) - Section 239, Code of Criminal Procedure, 1973 (CrPC) - Section 482; Constitution of India - Article 12, Constitution of India - Article 311, Constitution of India - Article 356; Indian Penal Code, 1860 (IPC) - Section 120B, Indian Penal Code, 1860 (IPC) - Section 166A, Indian Penal Code, 1860 (IPC) - Section 166B, Indian Penal Code, 1860 (IPC) - Section 201, Indian Penal Code, 1860 (IPC) - Section 354, Indian Penal Code, 1860 (IPC) - Section 354A, Indian Penal Code, 1860 (IPC) - Section 354B, Indian Penal Code, 1860 (IPC) - Section 354C, Indian Penal Code, 1860 (IPC) - Section 354D, Indian Penal Code, 1860 (IPC) - Section 370, Indian Penal Code, 1860 (IPC) - Section 375, Indian Penal Code, 1860 (IPC) - Section 376A, Indian Penal Code, 1860 (IPC) - Section 376AB, Indian Penal Code, 1860 (IPC) - Section 376C, Indian Penal Code, 1860 (IPC) - Section 376D, Indian Penal Code, 1860 (IPC) - Section 376DA, Indian Penal Code, 1860 (IPC) - Section 376DB, Indian Penal Code, 1860 (IPC) - Section 409, Indian Penal Code, 1860 (IPC) - Section 419, Indian Penal Code, 1860 (IPC) - Section 420, Indian Penal Code, 1860 (IPC) - Section 467, Indian Penal Code, 1860 (IPC) - Section 468, Indian Penal Code, 1860 (IPC) - Section 471, Indian Penal Code, 1860 (IPC) - Section 509; Prevention Of Corruption Act, 1988 - Section 7, Prevention Of Corruption Act, 1988 - Section 11, Prevention Of Corruption Act, 1988 - Section 13, Prevention Of Corruption Act, 1988 - Section 13(1), Prevention Of Corruption Act, 1988 - Section 13(2), Prevention Of Corruption Act, 1988 - Section 15, Prevention Of Corruption Act, 1988 - Section 19, Prevention Of Corruption Act, 1988 - Section 19(1)

Hon'ble Judges/Coram: B.R. Gavai and J.B. Pardiwala, JJ.

Equivalent Citation: AIR2023SC3811, 2023ALLMR (Cri)3108,2023/ INSC/682,2023(3) RCR(Criminal) 836

Number of Pages in the Original Judgment: 20

Case Reference:

Parkash Singh Badal and Ors. v. State of Punjab and Ors. MANU/SC/ 5415/2006; Kamal Shivaji Pokarnekar v. The State of Maharashtra and Ors. MANU/SC/0180/2019; Station House Officer, CBI/ACB/Bangalore v. B.A. Srinivasan and Ors. MANU/SC/1676/2019; S.K. Miglani v. State NCT of Delhi MANU/SC/0628/2019; Gokulchand Dwarkadas Morarka v. The King MANU/PR/0001/1948; K. Ch. Prasad v. J. Vanalatha Devi and Ors. MANU/ SC/0237/1987; Kalicharan Mahapatra v. State of Orissa MANU/SC/0473/ 1998

Case Note:

Criminal - Quashing of proceedings - Sections 120-B read with Section 420, 468 and 471 of the Indian Penal Code, 1860 (IPC); Section 197 of the Code of Criminal Procedure, 1973 (CrPC) - Present appeal arises from the judgment passed by a learned Single Judge of the High Court by which the High Court rejected the petition and thereby declined to quash the criminal proceedings instituted against the Appellant for the offence punishable under Sections 120-B read with Section 420, 468 and 471 of IPC - Whether the Appellant, serving in his capacity as an Assistant General Manager, State Bank of India, Overseas Bank, is removable from his office save by or with the sanction of the Government so as to make Section 197 of the CrPC applicable and that is it permissible for the Special Court (CBI) to proceed against the Appellant for the offences punishable under the IPC despite the fact that the sanction under Section 19 of the PC Act, 1988 to prosecute the Appellant for the offences under the PC Act, 1988, is not on record as the same came to be declined?

Facts:

The Appellant (Original Accused No. 2) at the relevant point of time was serving as an Assistant General Manager, State Bank of India, Overseas Bank (Bank), Hyderabad. He is alleged to have conspired with other co-Accused to cheat the Bank by sanctioning a corporate loan of Rs. 22.50 crore in favour of Sven Genetech Limited, Secunderabad (Original Accused No. 1). Appellant vehemently submitted that the sanction under Section 197 of the CrPC is mandatory to prosecute the Appellant for the offences Under Sections 120-B, 420, 468 and 471 respectively of the Indian Penal Code.

He would submit that as sanction to prosecute the Appellant under the provisions of the PC Act, 1988 came to be declined, the Appellant cannot now be prosecuted for the offences under Indian Penal Code without valid sanction Under Section 197 of the CrPC.

Held, while dismissing the appeal

1. Section 197 of the CrPC provides that, when any person who is or was a public servant, not removable from his office save by or with the sanction of the Central Government or State Government is Accused of any offence alleged to have been committed by him while acting or purporting to act in the discharge of his official duties, no Court shall take cognizance of such offence, except with the previous sanction of the appropriate Government. [40]

2. Sub-section (1) of Section 197 of the CrPC shows that sanction for prosecution is required where any person who is or was a Judge or Magistrate or a public servant not removable from his office save by or with the sanction of the Government is Accused of any offence alleged to have been committed by him while acting or purporting to act in discharge of his official duty. Article 311 of the Constitution lays down that no person, who is a member of a civil service of the Union or State or holds a civil post under the Union or State, shall be removed by an authority subordinate to that by which he was appointed. It, therefore, follows that protection of Sub-section (1) of Section 197 of CrPC is available only to such public servants whose appointing authority is the Central Government or the State Government and not to every public servant. [41]

3. The Appellant was serving as an Assistant General Manager, State Bank of India, Overseas Bank at Hyderabad. State Bank of India is a Nationalised Bank. Although a person working in a Nationalised Bank is a public servant, yet the provisions of Section 197 of the CrPC would not be attracted at all as Section 197 is attracted only in cases where the public servant is such who is not removable from his service save by or with the sanction of the Government. It is not disputed that the Appellant is not holding a post where he could not be removed from service except by or with the sanction of the Government. In this view of the matter, even if it is alleged that the Appellant herein is a public servant, still the provisions of Section 197 of the CrPC are not attracted at all. [45]

4. It is pertinent to note that, the banking sector being governed by the Reserve Bank of India and considered as a limb of the State Under Article 12 of the Constitution and also by virtue of Section 46A of the

Banking Regulation Act, 1949, the Appellant herein is deemed to be a "public servant' for the purpose of provisions under the PC Act, 1988. However, the same cannot be extended to the IPC. Assuming for a moment that the Appellant should be considered as a "public servant" for the Indian Penal Code sanction also, the protection available under Section 197 of the CrPC is not available to the Appellant herein since, the conditions in built under Section 197 of the CrPC are not fulfilled. [49]

5. Unfortunately, in the case on hand, the High Court also missed or overlooked the aforesaid aspect and confined its adjudication as to whether the acts alleged of the Appellant were in discharge of the official duty. [50]

6. There can be no thumb Rule that, in a prosecution before the court of Special Judge, the previous sanction Under Section 19 of the PC Act, 1988 would invariably be the only pre-requisite. There is a material difference between the statutory requirements of Section 19 of the PC Act, 1988 on one hand, and Section 197 of the CrPC, on the other. In the prosecution for the offences exclusively under the PC Act, 1988, sanction is mandatory qua the public servant. In cases under the general penal law against the public servant, the necessity (or otherwise) of sanction under Section 197 of the CrPC depends on the factual aspects. The test in the latter case is of the "nexus" between the act of commission or omission and the official duty of the public servant. To commit an offence punishable under law can never be a part of the official duty of a public servant. It is too simplistic an approach to adopt and to reject the necessity of sanction under Section 197 of the CrPC on such reasoning. The "safe and sure test", is to ascertain if the omission or neglect to commit the act complained of would have made the public servant answerable for the charge of dereliction of his official duty. He may have acted "in excess of his duty", but if there is a "reasonable connection" between the impugned act and the performance of the official duty, the protective umbrella of Section 197 of the CrPC cannot be denied, so long as the discharge of official duty is not used as a cloak for illicit acts. [59]

7. Appeal dismissed. [61]

Disposition: Appeal Dismissed.

• • •

CHAPTER II

State of Karnataka Lokayukta Police vs. S. Subbegowda (03.08.2023 – SC) : MANU/SC/0825/2023

Relative Section:

Code of Criminal Procedure, 1973 (CrPC) - Section 227, Code of Criminal Procedure, 1973 (CrPC) - Section 239, Code of Criminal Procedure, 1973 (CrPC) - Section 465, Code of Criminal Procedure, 1973 (CrPC) - Section 465(1), Code of Criminal Procedure, 1973 (CrPC) - Section 482; Prevention Of Corruption Act, 1988 - Section 4, Prevention Of Corruption Act, 1988 - Section 7, Prevention Of Corruption Act, 1988 - Section 11, Prevention Of Corruption Act, 1988 - Section 13, Prevention Of Corruption Act, 1988 - Section 13(1), Prevention Of Corruption Act, 1988 - Section 13(2), Prevention Of Corruption Act, 1988 - Section 15, Prevention Of Corruption Act, 1988 - Section 19, Prevention Of Corruption Act, 1988 - Section 19(1), Prevention Of Corruption Act, 1988 - Section 19(3), Prevention Of Corruption Act, 1988 - Section 19(4)

Hon'ble Judges/Coram: Aniruddha Bose and Bela M. Trivedi, JJ.

Equivalent Citation: AIR2023SC3770, 2023(3) AKR 854, 2023(3) Crimes175(SC), 2023/INSC/669,2023 (3) KLJ921, 2023(3)RCR(Criminal)802, 2023(3)RLW2679(SC)

Number of Pages in the Original Judgment: 9

Case Reference: Nanjappa v. State of Karnataka MANU/SC/0788/2015; State of Madhya Pradesh v. Bhooraji and Ors. MANU/SC/0481/2001; Shamnsaheb M. Multtani v. State of Karnataka MANU /SC /0047 /2001

Case Note:

Criminal - Discharge - Validity of sanction - Sections 13(1)(e), 13(2), 19(1), 19(3) and 19(4) of Prevention of Corruption Act, 1988 and Sections 227, 239 and 482 of Code of Criminal Procedure, 1973 - Respondent was working as Executive Engineer in Urban Water Supply and Drainage Board - Case was registered against Respondent for offence under Section 13(1)(e) read with Section 13(2) of Act - On completion of investigation, Investigating Officer had sent papers to State Government seeing sanction to prosecute Respondent as required in Section 19(1) of Act - Government had accorded requisite sanction by issuing Government order - Thereafter charge sheet came to be filed wherein it was alleged that Respondent had abused his position as public servant, had indulged into corrupt practices - Respondent-Accused filed application under Section 227 read with 239 of Code seeking his discharge from case contending, that sanction under Section 19(1) of Act was issued by Government without any application of mind- Said application came to be dismissed by trial court, thereafter Respondent preferred Criminal Revision Petition before High Court - High Court directed trial court to consider documents made available by Respondent during investigation and produced by prosecution - In view of said order passed by High Court, Respondent-Accused again filed application for discharge - Pertinently, Respondent did not press for said application by submitting memo and stating therein that Court may proceed to frame charge against him - Trial court thereafter framed charge against Respondent-Accused and prosecution thereafter examined seventeen witnesses and in midst of trial Respondent-Accused again filed third application under Section 227 of Code seeking his discharge from case on ground that State Government had no jurisdiction to accord sanction to prosecute Respondent under Section 19(1) of Act - Trial court dismissed said application by passing detailed order - Aggrieved Respondent filed Criminal Petition under Section 482 of Code before High Court, which came to be allowed by High Court - Hence, present appeal - Whether High Court in exercise of its powers under Section 482 of Code could have discharged Respondent-Accused from charges levelled against him for offences under Section 13(1)(e) punishable under Section 13(2) of Act, despite fact that Accused had not pressed for his second application for discharge by submitting Memo and despite fact that after framing of charge by Special Court, trial had proceeded further and prosecution had examined witnesses in support of its case and High Court in criminal petition filed under Section 482 of Code could reverse findings recorded by Special Court with regard to validity of sanction.

Facts:

The Respondent was working as an Executive Engineer in the Urban Water Supply and Drainage Board. On the basis of the Source Report submitted by the then Deputy Superintendent of Police, a case came to be registered against the Respondent for the offence under Section 13(1)(e) read with Section 13(2) of the said Act. It was alleged, that the Respondent-Accused during his tenure in the office as an Executive Engineer had amassed the wealth disproportionate to his known sources of income. On the completion of the investigation, the Investigating Officer had sent the papers to the State Government seeking sanction to prosecute the Respondent as required in Section 19(1) of the said Act. The Government on the basis of the material placed before it, had accorded the requisite sanction by issuing the Government order. Thereafter the chargesheet came to be filed in the Court wherein it was alleged that Respondent had abused his position as a public servant, had indulged into corrupt practices. The Respondent-Accused filed an application under Section 227 read with 239 of Code of Criminal Procedure seeking his discharge from the case contending, that neither the contents of the Source Report nor the other documents constituted any offence as alleged, and that the sanction under Section 19(1) of the said Act was issued by the Government without any application of mind. The said application came to be dismissed by the trial court. Being aggrieved by the said order, the Respondent preferred a Criminal Revision Petition before the High Court. The said petition came to be disposed of by the High Court directing the trial court to consider the documents made available by the Respondent during the investigation and produced by the prosecution with the chargesheet, while framing the charge. In view of the said order passed by the High Court, the Respondent-Accused again filed an application under Sections 227 and 239 of Code of Criminal Procedure before the trial court seeking his discharge from the case by contending, that the sanction order passed by the Government lacked application of mind. Pertinently, the Respondent did not press for the said application by submitting a memo and stating therein that the Court may proceed to frame charge against him. The trial court thereafter framed the charge against the Respondent-Accused for the offence of criminal misconduct under Section 13(1)(e) punishable under Section 13(2) of the said Act. The prosecution thereafter examined as many as seventeen witnesses in support of its case, and in the midst of the trial the Respondent-Accused again filed third application under Section 227 of Code of Criminal Procedure seeking his discharge from the case on the ground that the State Government had no jurisdiction to accord the sanction to prosecute the Respondent under Section 19(1) of the said Act. The trial court dismissed the said application by passing a detailed order holding, that the third successive application filed by the Respondent-Accused for the discharge from the case, when the evidence of seventeen witnesses had been recorded and when the contention based on the sanction was already rejected by the Court earlier, was liable to be dismissed. The aggrieved Respondent filed the Criminal Petition under Section 482 of Code of Criminal Procedure before the High Court, which came to be allowed by the High Court vide the impugned order.

Held, while allowing the appeal:

(i) After having not succeeded in the first application seeking discharge under Section 227 of Code of Criminal Procedure, in which the Petitioner had raised the issue of sanction by contending that the sanction was accorded by the Government under Section 19(1) of the said Act without any application of mind, the Respondent- Accused had filed the second application again seeking his discharge under Section 227 of Code of Criminal Procedure by raising the issue of sanction by contending, inter alia, that the sanction order was passed mechanically by the Government and that the Investigating Officer had suppressed the material produced by the Respondent offering satisfactory explanations to the assets acquired by him. Admittedly, the second application was not pressed for by the Respondent by submitting the Memo, wherein it was stated that the Court may proceed to frame charge against him. Thus, by submitting the said Memo, the Respondent-Accused had specifically not pressed for his contention with regard to the validity of sanction or error in granting the sanction by the Government, and he specifically requested the Court to proceed further with the framing of charge. Considering the said memo, the trial court framed the charge, and the prosecution examined as many as seventeen witnesses in support of its case. At that stage, the Respondent submitted the third application which was in the nature of interlocutory application again seeking the discharge under Section 227 of Code of Criminal Procedure on the ground that there was an error in the sanction order, the Government being not competent to grant the sanction under Section 19(1) of the said Act. The said application having been dismissed by the trial court, the High Court could not and should not have entertained the petition under Section 482 of Code of Criminal Procedure, which was in the nature of revision application, and reversed the findings recorded by the trial court, in view of Sub-section (3) read with Sub-section (4) of Section 19 of the said Act. [7]

(ii) In the instant case, the Special Judge proceeded with the trial, on the second application for discharge filed by the Respondent having not been pressed for by him. The Special Judge, while dismissing the third application filed by the Respondent seeking discharge after examination of seventeen witnesses by the prosecution, specifically held that the sanction accorded by the government which was a superior authority to the Water Supply Board, of which the Respondent was an employee, was proper and valid. Such findings recorded by the Special Judge could not have been and should not have been reversed or altered by the High Court in the petition filed by the Respondent challenging the said order of the Special Judge, in view of the specific bar contained in Sub-section (3) of Section 19, and that too without recording any opinion as to how a failure of justice had in fact been occasioned to the Respondent-Accused as contemplated in the said Sub-section (3). As a matter of fact, neither the Respondent had pleaded nor the High Court opined whether any failure of justice had occasioned to the Respondent, on account of error if any, occurred in granting the sanction by the authority. [14]

(iii) As a matter of fact, such an interlocutory application seeking discharge in the midst of trial would also not be maintainable. Once the cognizance was taken by the Special Judge and the charge was framed against the Accused, the trial could neither have been stayed nor scuttled in the midst of it in view of Section 19 (3) of the said Act. In the instant case, though the issue of validity of sanction was raised at the earlier point of time, the same was not pressed for. The only stage open to the Respondent-Accused in that situation was to raise the said issue at the final arguments in the trial in accordance with law. [15]

Ratio Decidendi : The stages of proceedings at which an Accused could raise the issue with regard to the validity of the sanction would be the stage when the Court takes cognizance of the offence, the stage when the charge is to be framed by the Court or at the stage when the trial is complete i.e., at the stage of final arguments in the trial.

Disposition: In Favour of State.

• • •

CHAPTER III

K.M. Mallaiah vs. State of Karnataka (10.02.2015 – SC): MANU /SC/0446/2015

Relative Section:

Prevention of Corruption Act, 1988 - Section 7; Prevention of Corruption Act, 1988 - Section 13(1);Prevention of Corruption Act, 1988 - Section 13(2)

Hon'ble Judges/Coram: Madan B. Lokur and R.K. Agrawal, JJ.

Equivalent Citation: 2015(2) RCR (Criminal) 117

Number of Pages in the Original Judgment: 3

Case Reference: nil

Case Note:

Criminal - Prevention of corruption - Sections 7 and 13(1)(d) read with Section 13(2) Prevention of Corruption Act, 1988 - Appellant convicted for accepting bribe in 2006 - Complainant died in 2011 - Micro tape recorder used in trap not adduced before trial court - PW1 did not hear conversation between Appellant and Complainant - Treated currency notes handled by Appellant lost - High Court upheld order of conviction - Whether the High Court erred in upholding the conviction of the Appellant

Facts

The Complainant alleged that the Appellant had asked for a bribe to sanction his pay for medical leave. A trap was laid in which the Complainant, in the presence of PW1 would pay the bribe, and the proceedings would be recorded by micro tape recorder. The trial court found the Appellant guilty. The High Court affirmed conviction. Hence, the present appeal.

Held, allowing the appeal

1. The micro tape recorder was not produced before the trial court, however, there is no finding given by the High Court in this regard. The High Court has considered only the examination-in-chief of PW1, but not his cross-examination to the effect that he did not hear the conversation between the Complainant, who died during pendency, and the Appellant. There is no evidence on record to indicate that the

Appellant had demanded a bribe from the Complainant. In the circumstances, the High Court erred in upholding the conviction of the Appellant.[12],[13] and[14]

•••

CHAPTER IV

Y. Balaji vs. Karthik Desari and Ors. (16.05.2023 – SC) : MANU/SC/0584/2023

Relative Section:

Arms Act 1959 - Section 25; Code of Criminal Procedure, 1973 (CrPC) - Section 160, Code of Criminal Procedure, 1973 (CrPC) - Section 161, Code of Criminal Procedure, 1973 (CrPC) - Section 164, Code of Criminal Procedure, 1973 (CrPC) - Section 173, Code of Criminal Procedure, 1973 (CrPC) - Section 173(2), Code of Criminal Procedure, 1973 (CrPC) - Section 173(8), Code of Criminal Procedure, 1973 (CrPC) - Section 216, Code of Criminal Procedure, 1973 (CrPC) - Section 482; Constitution of India - Article 20(3), Constitution of India - Article 21, Constitution of India - Article 22; Indian Evidence Act, 1872 - Section 65B; Indian Penal Code, 1860 (IPC) - Section 34, Indian Penal Code, 1860 (IPC) - Section 109, Indian Penal Code, 1860 (IPC) - Section 120B, Indian Penal Code, 1860 (IPC) - Section 201, Indian Penal Code, 1860 (IPC) - Section 302, Indian Penal Code, 1860 (IPC) - Section 406, Indian Penal Code, 1860 (IPC) - Section 419, Indian Penal Code, 1860 (IPC) - Section 420, Indian Penal Code, 1860 (IPC) - Section 465, Indian Penal Code, 1860 (IPC) - Section 467, Indian Penal Code, 1860 (IPC) - Section 471, Indian Penal Code, 1860 (IPC) - Section 506(1); Prevention Of Corruption Act, 1988 - Section 7, Prevention Of Corruption Act, 1988 - Section 12, Prevention Of Corruption Act, 1988 - Section 13, Prevention Of Corruption Act, 1988 - Section 13(1), Prevention Of Corruption Act, 1988 - Section 13(2); Prevention Of Money-laundering Act, 2002 - Section 2(1), Prevention Of Money-laundering Act, 2002 - Section 3, Prevention Of Money-laundering Act, 2002 - Section 3(2), Prevention Of Money-laundering Act, 2002 - Section 8, Prevention Of Money-laundering Act, 2002 - Section 50, Prevention Of Money-laundering Act, 2002 - Section 50(2), Prevention Of Money-laundering Act, 2002 - Section 63, Prevention Of Money-laundering Act, 2002 - Section 66(2)

Hon'ble Judges/Coram: Krishna Murari and V. Ramasubramanian, JJ.

Equivalent Citation: AIR2023SC3171, 2023/INSC/542, 2023(3)MLJ(Crl)113, 2023 (2) MWN (CR.) 679, [2023]179SCL49(SC)

Number of Pages in the Original Judgment: 42

Case Reference:

Vinay Tyagi v. Irshad Ali and Ors. MANU/SC/1101/2012; Union of India v. Ganpati Dealcom Private Limited MANU/SC/1028/2022; Central Board of Dawoodi Bohra Community v. State of Maharashtra MANU/SC/0120/2023; Janata Dal v. H.S. Chowdhary and Ors. MANU/SC/0532/1992; Simranjit Singh Mann v. Union of India (UOI) and Ors. MANU/SC/0058/1993; Bihta Co-operative Development Cane Marketing Union Ltd. and Ors. v. The Bank of Bihar and Ors. MANU/SC/0260/1966; Shauqin Singh and Ors. v. Desa Singh and Ors. MANU/SC/0388/1969; Kantaru Rajeevaru* v. Indian Young Lawyers Association and Ors. MANU/SC/0443/2020; Asgar Ali v. The State of Jammu and Kashmir and Ors. MANU/SC/1116/2021; Badrinath v. Government of Tamil Nadu and Ors. MANU/SC/0624/2000; State of Punjab v. Davinder Pal Singh Bhullar and Ors. MANU/SC/1476/2011; Management of Northern Railway Co-operative Society Ltd. v. Industrial Tribunal, Rajasthan, Jaipur and Ors. MANU/SC/0221/1967; P. Dharamaraj v. Shanmugam MANU/SC/1119/2022; Sakshi and Ors. v. Union of India (UOI) and Ors. MANU/SC/0523/2004; Enforcement Directorate v. Gagandeep Singh MANU/DE/0535/2022; Vijay Madanlal Choudhary v. Union of India MANU/SC/0924/2022; Central Board of Dawoodi Bohra Community and Ors. v. State of Maharashtra and Ors. MANU/SC/1069/2004

Case Note:

Criminal -De novo investigation -Quashing of summons - Sections 34, 406 and 420 of Indian Penal Code, 1860, Sections 2(1)(u) and 3 of Prevention of Money-Laundering Act, 2002, Section 173(8) of Code of Criminal Procedure, 1973 and Section 65B of Indian Evidence Act, 1872- High Court ordered de novo investigation in petition filed at instance of complainant alleging that accused person received money for securing job of Conductor for his son and thereby committed offence punishable under Sections 406 and 420 read with Section 34 of Code - Thereafter, writ petitions filed before High Court challenging summons issued by ED - High Court quashed summons on ground that one of four calendar cases had already been quashed by High Court on basis of Joint Compromise Memo - High Court further refused to extend time for completion of investigation - Hence, present appeals - Whether High Court erred in ordering de novo investigation in alleged offence, quashing summons issued by ED and in refusing to extend time for completion of investigation.

Facts:

The High Court passed an order allowing the petition filed by complainant and ordered a de novo investigation in petition filed alleging that accused person received a sumfor securing the job of a Conductor for his son and that he and his accomplices committed offences punishable under Sections 406 and 420 read with Section 34 Indian Penal Code. Thereafter, three writ petitions came to be filed, by accused persons challenging the summons issued by ED. These writ petitions were allowed by the High Court by an order primarily on the ground that one of the four calendar cases had already been quashed by the High Court on the basis of a Joint Compromise Memo and that further proceedings in the other calendar cases had been stayed by the High Court. The High Court further refused to extend the time for completion of investigation.

Held, while disposing off the appeals:

(i) Though the original petition and the arguments recorded in the impugned order did not reflect one particular ground, the operative portion of the impugned order allows de novo investigation on a ground not raised in the petition. In the impugned order, it was recorded by the High Court that as per the affidavit filed by the Investigating Officer, the investigating agency had seized the register used for entering interview marks and sent the same to the Forensic Department for analysis to find out the manipulations and that the Final Report under Section 173(8) of the Code was filed even before the receipt of the report of the Forensic Department. It was on this contention that the High Court thought fit to order de novo investigation not only in the case in which complainant sought de novo investigation but also in all the criminal cases. What was interesting was that the order directing de novo investigation in all the three cases, had actually inured to the benefit of the Accused, but the High Court put it on the ground that the credibility of the investigation should not be eroded. In fact, the Accused did not seek de novo investigation on the ground of slackness on the part of the Investigating Officer, but it was complainant who sought it, with the able assistance of the Investigating Officer.[19]

(ii) By issuing the direction, the High Court not only directed the wiping out of the investigation carried out so far, but virtually wiped out even the judgment of this Court passed in Criminal Appeal.[22]

(iii) The High Court had not quashed the summons issued by ED. The High Court had merely injuncted ED from proceeding further till the clog on the cases relating to the predicate offences was removed.[67]

(iv) Even if an intangible property was derived as a result of criminal activity relating to a scheduled offence, it becomes proceeds of crime under Section 2(1)(u). This court was not impressed with the contention that the investigation by ED was triggered without any foundational/jurisdictional facts. In our view, the allegations in the FIR point out to involvement of persons in criminal activity relating to scheduled offences, the generation as well as laundering of the proceeds of crime within the meaning of Section 3. This was in view of the fact that wherever there are allegations of corruption, there was acquisition of proceeds of crime which itself tantamount to money-laundering.[104]

(v) Section 65B concerns the admissibility of electronic records. Without certification, ED may not be able to use those electronic records in evidence, in the prosecution under PMLA. But it did not mean that they could not even have a look at the electronic record.[123]

(vi) When a petition for extension of time was moved, the Court rejected on the ground that the prayer had become infructuous. Therefore, worried about the fate of further investigation, the victim had come up with the appeal. But the worry of the Appellant is baseless. Merely because the High Court had not granted extension of time, it does not mean that the direction to conduct further investigation had become infructuous. On the contrary, a Final Report had already been filed under Section 173(8) of the Code.[125]

• • •

CHAPTER V

A. Srinivasulu vs. The State Rep. by the Inspector of Police (15.06.2023 – SC) : MANU/SC/0723/2023

Relative Section:

Code of Criminal Procedure, 1898 (CrPC) - Section 190, Code of Criminal Procedure, 1898 (CrPC) - Section 209, Code of Criminal Procedure, 1898 (CrPC) - Section 337, Code of Criminal Procedure, 1898 (CrPC) - Section 338; Code of Criminal Procedure, 1973 (CrPC) - Section 161, Code of Criminal Procedure, 1973 (CrPC) - Section 164, Code of Criminal Procedure, 1973 (CrPC) - Section 195(1), Code of Criminal Procedure, 1973 (CrPC) - Section 197, Code of Criminal Procedure, 1973 (CrPC) - Section 197(1), Code of Criminal Procedure, 1973 (CrPC) - Section 306, Code of Criminal Procedure, 1973 (CrPC) - Section 306(1), Code of Criminal Procedure, 1973 (CrPC) - Section 306(4), Code of Criminal Procedure, 1973 (CrPC) - Section 307, Code of Criminal Procedure, 1973 (CrPC) - Section 308, Code of Criminal Procedure, 1973 (CrPC) - Section 313, Code of Criminal Procedure, 1973 (CrPC) - Section 326, Code of Criminal Procedure, 1973 (CrPC) - Section 475; Government Of India Act, 1935 - Section 270(1); Indian Evidence Act, 1872 - Section 73, Indian Evidence Act, 1872 - Section 114, Indian Evidence Act, 1872 - Section 133, Indian Penal Code, 1860 (IPC) - Section 21, Indian Penal Code, 1860 (IPC) - Section 109, Indian Penal Code, 1860 (IPC) - Section 120B, Indian Penal Code, 1860 (IPC) - Section 193, Indian Penal Code, 1860 (IPC) - Section 409, Indian Penal Code, 1860 (IPC) - Section 420, Indian Penal Code, 1860 (IPC) - Section 467, Indian Penal Code, 1860 (IPC) - Section 468, Indian Penal Code, 1860 (IPC) - Section 471, Indian Penal Code, 1860 (IPC) - Section 477A; Prevention Of Corruption Act, 1988 - Section 2(c), Prevention Of Corruption Act, 1988 - Section 5, Prevention Of Corruption Act, 1988 - Section 5(1), Prevention Of Corruption Act, 1988 - Section 5(2), Prevention Of Corruption Act, 1988 - Section 13(1), Prevention Of Corruption Act, 1988 - Section 13(2), Prevention Of Corruption Act, 1988 - Section 19(1)

Hon'ble Judges/Coram: V. Ramasubramanian and Pankaj Mithal, JJ.

Equivalent Citation: 2023 (2) ALT (Crl.) 317 (A.P.), 2023 (2) MWN (CR.) 337, 2023(3)RLW1964(SC)

Number of Pages in the Original Judgment: 40

Case Reference:

Dr. Hori Ram Singh v. Emperor MANU/FE/0001/1939; Matajog Dobey v. H.C. Bhari MANU/SC/0071/1955; State of Orissa through Kumar Raghvendra Singh and Ors. v. Ganesh Chandra Jew MANU/SC/0264/2004; K. Kalimuthu v. State MANU/SC/0248/2005; Rakesh Kumar Mishra v. The State of Bihar and Ors. MANU /SC /0200/2006; Devinder Singh and Ors. v. State of Punjab through CBI MANU/SC/0450/2016; D. Devaraja v. Owais Sabeer Hussain MANU/SC/0490/2020; Parkash Singh Badal and Ors. v. State of Punjab and Ors. MANU/SC/5415/2006; Bangaru Laxman v. State (through CBI) and Ors. MANU/SC/1409/2011; Harshad S. Mehta and Ors. v. The State of Maharashtra MANU/SC/0540/2001; P.C. Mishra v. State (C.B.I.) and Ors. MANU/SC/0232/2014; State through CBI, Chennai v. V. Arul Kumar MANU/SC/0632/2016; A. Deivendran v. State of T.N. MANU/SC/1851/1997; Suresh Chandra Bahri v. State of Bihar and Ors. MANU/SC/0500/1994; Sardar Iqbal Singh v. State (Delhi Administration) and Ors. MANU/SC/0131/1977; Yakub Abdul Razak Memon and Ors. v. State of Maharashtra through CBI, Bombay MANU/SC/0268/2013; Sarwan Singh v. The State of Punjab MANU/SC/0038/1957; Ravinder Singh v. State of Haryana MANU/SC/0199/1975; M.O. Shamsudhin v. State of Kerala MANU/SC/0677/1995

Case Note:

Criminal - Conviction - Legality -Section 120B read with Sections 420, 468, Section 471 read with Section 468 and Section 193 of Indian Penal Code, 1860 (IPC) and Section 13(2) read with Section 13(1)(d) of the PC Act - Appeals arise out of a common judgment passed by the High Court confirming the conviction of the Appellants for various offences under the Indian Penal Code, 1860 and the Prevention of Corruption Act, 1988 - Whether Appellants are to be acquitted of all the charges?

Facts: while allowing the appeal

The case of the prosecution was that A-1 to A-7 entered into a criminal conspiracy to cheat BHEL in the matter of award of contract for the construction of desalination plants. Seven persons, four of whom were officers of BHEL, Trichy (a Public Sector Undertaking), and the remaining three engaged in private enterprise, were charged by the Inspector of Police, through a final report, for alleged offences Under Section 120B read with

Sections 420, 468, Section 471 read with Section 468 and Section 193 of IPC and Section 13(2) read with Section 13(1)(d) of the PC Act. Cognizance was taken by the Principal Special Judge for CBI cases. During the pendency of trial, two of the Accused, namely, A-5 and A-6 died. By a judgment, the Special Court acquitted A-2 and convicted A-1, A-3, A-4 and A-7 for various offences. These four convicted persons filed three appeals in Criminal Appeal, on the file of the Madurai Bench of the Madras High Court. By a common judgment the High Court dismissed the appeals, forcing A-1, A-3, A-4 and A-7 to come up with four criminal appeals. However, during the pendency of the above appeals, A-3 (R. Thiagarajan) died and hence Criminal Appeal filed by him was dismissed as abated.

Held, while allowing the appeal

1.There is no dispute about the fact that A-1 to A-4, being officers of a company coming within the description contained in the Twelfth item of Section 21 of the IPC, were 'public servants' within the definition of the said expression under Section 21 of the IPC. A-1 to A-4 were also public servants within the meaning of the expression Under Section 2(c)(iii) of the PC Act. Therefore, there is a requirement of previous sanction both Under Section 197(1) of the IPC and Under Section 19(1) of the PC Act, for prosecuting A-1 to A-4 for the offences punishable under the IPC and the PC Act. [29]

2. In D. Devaraja v. Owais Sabeer Hussain, this Court explained that sanction is required not only for acts done in the discharge of official duty but also required for any act purported to be done in the discharge of official duty and/or act done under colour of or in excess of such duty or authority. This Court also held that to decide whether sanction is necessary, the test is whether the act is totally unconnected with official duty or whether there is a reasonable connection with the official duty. [42]

3. To recapitulate, the allegations against A-1 are (i) that by entering into a criminal conspiracy to cheat BHEL and award the tender to A-5's firm and by instructing PW-16 to go in for limited tenders without following the procedure of pre-qualification of prospective tenderers and without selecting any one from the approved list of contractors, he committed various offences punishable under the Indian Penal Code; and (ii) that by abusing his official position and awarding the contract to A-5, he caused a wrongful loss to the tune of Rs. 4.32 crores to BHEL. [81]

4. For proving the allegations with regard to the criminal conspiracy and for establishing that A-1 decided to go in for Restricted Tender for the purpose of awarding the contract to a chosen firm and also for showing that

A-1 directed the inclusion of four bogus firms, the prosecution relied upon its star witness, namely PW-16. But PW-16 was the first-named Accused in the FIR, who later turned approver by giving a confession statement. [82]

5. Present Court has laid down two tests in Sarwan Singh v. State of Punjab , to be satisfied before accepting the evidence of an approver. The first is that the approver is a reliable witness and the second is that his statement should be corroborated with sufficient evidence. Again, in Ravinder Singh v. State of Haryana, this Court pointed out that, "an approver is a most unworthy friend" and that he having bargained for his immunity, must prove his worthiness for credibility in court. [83]

6. Section 133 of the Indian Evidence Act, 1872 declares an accomplice to be a competent witness and that a conviction is not illegal merely because it proceeds upon the uncorroborated testimony of an accomplice. However, while considering the import of Section 133. this Court held in M.O. Shamsudhin v. State of Kerala, that the court is bound to take note of a precautionary provision contained in Illustration (b) to Section 114 of the Evidence Act, which provides that an accomplice is unworthy of credit unless he is corroborated in material particulars. [84]

7. The Trial Court and the High Court came to the conclusion that the names of two big companies were included in Exhibit P-26 chit only to lend credibility to the process adopted. But it was on record through the statement of PW-4, Manager of L&T Company that a tender enquiry was received by them from BHEL. If the inclusion of the names of those two companies were intended to be a make belief affair, A-1 would not have taken the risk of sending the letter and that too to a company like L&T. Therefore, present Court is of the view, (i) that the evidence of PW-16 was not worthy of credit; (ii) that even assuming that it has some credibility, his statement that "he recommended the contract to be given to A-5 not because of A-1's interest", made the whole edifice upon which the case of the prosecution was built, collapse; and (iii) that there was no other evidence to connect A-1 with the commission of these offences. [102]

8. In fact, the only person found by both the Courts to be guilty of the offence Under Section 120B was A-1. Therefore, an argument was advanced that a single person cannot be held guilty of criminal conspiracy. But this contention was repelled by the Courts on the ground that PW-16 was the second person with whom A-1 had entered into a conspiracy. In other words, the reasoning adopted by the Trial Court and the High Court was that only A-1 and PW-16 were part of the conspiracy. Such a reasoning

was a huge climbdown from the original charge that A-1 to A-7 entered into a criminal conspiracy, to cause wrongful loss to BHEL and to confer a wrongful gain to A-5 to A-7. Once an offence of Section 120B is not made out against A-5 to A-7, the very foundation for the prosecution becomes shaky. Therefore, the conviction of A-1 for the offences Under Section 120B read with Sections 420, 468, Section 471 read with Section 468 and Section 193 of IPC and Section 13(2) read with Section 13(1)(d) of the PC Act cannot be sustained. [103]

9. Present Court is surprised that A-1 was found guilty of an offence Under Section 193 of IPC. Section 193 of IPC applies only to false evidence given in any stage of a judicial proceeding or the fabrication of false evidence for the purpose of being used in any stage of a judicial proceeding. The allegation against A-1 was not even remotely linked to any of the Explanations Under Section 193 of IPC . Therefore, the judgment of the Trial Court and that of the High Court convicting A-1 for the aforesaid offences and sentencing him to imprisonment of varying terms and fines of different amounts are liable to be reversed. [104]

10. As can be seen from the judgment of the Trial Court, A-4 was convicted for the offences Under Section 109 read with Section 420, 468 of IPC, Section 471 read with 468 of IPC and Section 193 of IPC. [105]

11. Interestingly, there was no allegation that either A-1 or A-3 or A-4 either gave false evidence or fabricated false evidence in any stage of a judicial proceeding, falling within any of the three Explanations Under Section 193. But unfortunately, the Trial Court found A-4 guilty of the offence Under Section 193, without there being any specific allegation in the charge-sheet and without there being any specific finding on merits. [107]

12. In fact, the prosecution had to stand or fall on the strength of the testimony of the Approver namely PW-16. But this is what PW-16 said about the role played by A-3 and A-4. [111]

13. A-4 had no role in choosing the tenderers, but entered the picture only after the offers were received from the tenderers. Admittedly, A-4 was subordinate to both PW-16 and A-3. [113]

14. The competent authority refused to grant sanction to prosecute A-3 and A-4 for the offences under the PC Act. The Trial Court and the High Court did not find A-4 as a co-conspirator, which is why he was not held guilty of the offence Under Section 120-B of IPC . Section 193 of IPC had been included completely out of context. [114]

15. The conviction of A-4 by the Trial Court as confirmed by the High Court is wholly unsustainable and is liable to be set aside. [115]

16. The High Court fortunately realised the pitfall in the reasoning of the Trial Court. But in an over-anxiety to somehow convict A-7, the High Court adopted a very peculiar route, namely that of undertaking the task of comparing the admitted signatures/ handwritings with the disputed ones under Section 73 of the Evidence Act. [130]

17. For invoking Section 73, there must first have been some signature or writing admitted or proved to the satisfaction of the Court, to have been written or made by that person. The Section empowers the Court also to direct any person present in Court to write any words or figures for the purpose of enabling the Court to compare the words or figures. [131]

18. There was no signature or writing available before the High Court, which had been admitted or proved to the satisfaction of the Court to have been written or made. The High Court did not also direct A-7 to write any words or figures for the purpose of enabling a comparison. Without following the procedure so prescribed in Section 73, the High Court invented a novel procedure, to uphold the conviction handed over by the Trial Court through a wrong reasoning. [132]

19. In the absence of either admission or proof of the admitted signatures, the High Court could not have resorted to Section 73 of the Evidence Act. [136]

20. The finding recorded by the Trial Court and the High Court as though A-7 committed forgery and cheating by making applications for the issue of demand drafts in the names of bogus firms is wholly unsustainable. [137]

21. The only connecting link pointed out against A-7 was the transfer of money to the total extent of Rs. 1,52,50,000 to the account of a firm of which he was a partner. This by itself will not constitute any offence. Therefore, the charge that A-7 abetted the commission of the crime by the other Accused, should also fail. This is especially so when A-5, whose proprietary concern bagged the contract, not only lost the contract but also allowed the bank guarantee to be invoked by BHEL and in addition, left a huge amount of Rs. 2.60 crores still with BHEL. Therefore, the conviction and sentence awarded to A-7 cannot be sustained. [138]

22. The judgment of the Special Court for CBI cases convicting the Appellants for various offences and the judgment of the High Court confirming the same are set aside. The Appellants are acquitted of all the

charges. Appeal allowed. [139]

Ratio Decidendi: Sanction is required not only for acts done in the discharge of official duty but also required for any act purported to be done under colour of or in excess of such duty or authority

Disposition: In Favour of Accused.

...

CHAPTER VI

Judgebir Singh and Ors. vs. National Investigation Agency (01.05.2023 – SC):MANU/SC/0501/2023

Relative Section:

Code of Criminal Procedure, 1898 (CrPC) - Section 167; Code of Criminal Procedure, 1973 (CrPC) - Section 2, Code of Criminal Procedure, 1973 (CrPC) - Section 57, Code of Criminal Procedure, 1973 (CrPC) - Section 167, Code of Criminal Procedure, 1973 (CrPC) - Section 167(2), Code of Criminal Procedure, 1973 (CrPC) - Section 170, Code of Criminal Procedure, 1973 (CrPC) - Section 173, Code of Criminal Procedure, 1973 (CrPC) - Section 173(2), Code of Criminal Procedure, 1973 (CrPC) - Section 173(4), Code of Criminal Procedure, 1973 (CrPC) - Section 173(5), Code of Criminal Procedure, 1973 (CrPC) - Section 173(8), Code of Criminal Procedure, 1973 (CrPC) - Section 175(5), Code of Criminal Procedure, 1973 (CrPC) - Section 193, Code of Criminal Procedure, 1973 (CrPC) - Section 209, Code of Criminal Procedure, 1973 (CrPC) - Section 268, Code of Criminal Procedure, 1973 (CrPC) - Section 309, Code of Criminal Procedure, 1973 (CrPC) - Section 438; Constitution of India - Article 21, Constitution of India - Article 22(2), Constitution of India - Article 32; Explosive Substances Act, 1908 - Section 4, Explosive Substances Act, 1908 - Section 5; Indian Penal Code, 1860 (IPC) - Section 34, Indian Penal Code, 1860 (IPC) - Section 109, Indian Penal Code, 1860 (IPC) - Section 120B, Indian Penal Code, 1860 (IPC) - Section 177, Indian Penal Code, 1860 (IPC) - Section 406, Indian Penal Code, 1860 (IPC) - Section 408, Indian Penal Code, 1860 (IPC) - Section 409, Indian Penal Code, 1860 (IPC) - Section 411, Indian Penal Code, 1860 (IPC) - Section 465, Indian Penal Code, 1860 (IPC) - Section 466, Indian Penal Code, 1860 (IPC) - Section 468, Indian Penal Code, 1860 (IPC) - Section 471; National Investigation Agency Act 2008 - Section 6, National Investigation Agency Act 2008 - Section 7, National Investigation Agency Act 2008 - Section 10, National Investigation Agency Act 2008 - Section 11, National Investigation Agency Act 2008 - Section 13, National Investigation Agency Act 2008 - Section 15, National Investigation Agency Act 2008 - Section 16, National

Investigation Agency Act 2008 - Section 16(1), National Investigation Agency Act 2008 - Section 18, National Investigation Agency Act 2008 - Section 22, National Investigation Agency Act 2008 - Section 22(2); Prevention Of Corruption Act, 1988 - Section 13(1), Prevention Of Corruption Act, 1988 - Section 13(2); Terrorist And Disruptive Activities (prevention) Act, 1987 - Section 20(4); Unlawful Activities (prevention) (recommendation And Sanction Of Prosecution) Rules, 2008 - Rule 3, Unlawful Activities (prevention) (recommendation And Sanction Of Prosecution) Rules, 2008 - Rule 4; Unlawful Activities (prevention) Act, 1967 - Section 2(1), Unlawful Activities (prevention) Act, 1967 - Section 17, Unlawful Activities (prevention) Act, 1967 - Section 18, Unlawful Activities (prevention) Act, 1967 - Section 18B, Unlawful Activities (prevention) Act, 1967 - Section 20, Unlawful Activities (prevention) Act, 1967 - Section 43D, Unlawful Activities (prevention) Act, 1967 - Section 43D(2), Unlawful Activities (prevention) Act, 1967 - Section 45, Unlawful Activities (prevention) Act, 1967 - Section 45(1)

Hon'ble Judges/Coram: Dr. D.Y. Chandrachud, C.J.I. and J.B. Pardiwala, J.

Equivalent Citation: 2023 (2) ALT (Crl.) 283 (A.P.), 2023/INSC/472, 2023(2)J.L.J.R.374, 2023(3)MLJ(Crl)1, 2023(2)PLJR384, 2023(3)RCR(Criminal)334

Number of Pages in the Original Judgment: 35
Case Reference:
Fakhrey Alam v. State of Uttar Pradesh MANU/SC/0251/2021; Abdul Azeez P.V. v. National Investigation Agency MANU/SC/1032/2014; Rambhai Nathabhai Gadhvi and Ors. v. State of Gujarat MANU/SC/0859/ 1997; Ashrafkhan and Ors. v. State of Gujarat MANU/SC/0790/2012; Bikramjit Singh v. The State of Punjab MANU/SC/0749/2020; Sanjay Dutt v. State through C.B.I., Bombay MANU/SC/0554/1994; Suresh Kumar Bhikamchand Jain v. State of Maharashtra and Ors. MANU/SC/0196/2013; Uday Mohanlal Acharya v. State of Maharashtra MANU/SC/0222/2001; Rakesh Kumar Paul v. State of Assam MANU/SC/0993/2017; Union of India (UOI) v. Nirala Yadav MANU/SC/0580/2014; Mohamed Iqbal Madar Sheikh and Ors. v. State of Maharashtra MANU/SC/1045/1996; Achpal and Ors. v. State of Rajasthan MANU/SC/1035/2018; Mahaveer Meghwal v. State of Rajasthan MANU/RH/0391/2018; Dinesh Dalmia v. C.B.I. MANU/ SC/7924/2007; Central Bureau of Investigation (CBI) v. R.S. Pai and Ors. MANU/SC/0246/2002; Narayan Rao v. The State of Andhra Pradesh

MANU/SC/0042/1957; Satya Narain Musadi and Ors. v. State of Bihar MANU/SC/0234/1979; K. Veeraswami v. Union of India (UOI) and Ors. MANU/SC/0610/1991; C.B.I. v. Ashok Kumar Aggarwal MANU/SC/1220/2013; Matabar Parida and Ors. v. State of Orissa MANU/SC/0157/1975; M. Ravindran v. The Intelligence Officer, Directorate of Revenue Intelligence MANU/SC/0788/2020; Union of India (UOI) and Ors. v. Thamisharasi and Ors. MANU/SC/0714/1995; Sayed Mohd. Ahmed Kazmi v. State, GNCTD and Ors. MANU/SC/0900/2012; Chitra Ramkrishna v. Central Bureau of Investigation, MANU/DE/3747/2022; Serious Fraud Investigation Office v. Rahul Modi and Ors. MANU/SC/0156/2022; Satish Kumar v. State of Punjab and Anr. MANU/SCOR/06591/2021; Jigar alias Jimmy Pravinchandra Aditya v. State of Gujarat reported in MANU/SC/1233/2022

Case Note:

Criminal - Default bail - Sanction to prosecute - Sections 167, 167(2), 173(2), 173(5) and 193 of Code of Criminal Procedure, 1973, Sections 17, 18, 18B, 20 and 43D of Unlawful Activities Act, 1967, Sections 4 and 5 of Explosive Substances Act, 1908 and Section 16 of National Investigation Agency Act, 2008 -FIR was registered against Accused for offences punishable under Sections 17, 18, 18B and 20 of Act, 1967 and Sections 4 and 5 of Act, 1908 - Additional Sessions Judge, extended period of completion of investigation thereafter, final under Section 173(2) of Code was presented before Court of Sub- Divisional Judicial Magistrate - NIA re-registeredinstant case under Sections 17, 18, 18B and 20 of UAPA and prosecution stood transferred to Special Court - Thereafter, District Magistrate, accorded sanction for prosecution under 1908 Act - Special Judge, NIA recorded that sanction to prosecute Accused persons for offences under 1908 Act had been accorded and sanction under UAPA was being awaited - Application for default bail under Section 167(2) of Code read with Section 43D of UAPA was filed before Special Judge NIA, essentially on ground that although chargesheet had been filed within extended period, yet same could be termed as incomplete because of want of sanction under UAPA - Special Court rejected application filed by Accused persons seeking default bail - Thereafter, Government accorded sanction for prosecution under UAPA - Appellants filed appeal before High Court against order rejecting default bail application which stand rejected - Hence, present appeal - Whether Accused was entitled to seek default bail under Section 167(2) of Code on ground that although chargesheet might have been filed within statutory time period yet chargesheet sans valid order of sanction passed by competent authority was no chargesheet in eye of law and cognizance of chargesheet was necessary to prevent Accused from seeking default bail and further error on part of investigating agency to file chargesheet for alleged offences in Court of Magistrate and not in Sessions or designated Court would by itself entitle Accused to seek default bail.

Facts:

An FIR was registered against Accused for offences punishable under Sections 17, 18, 18B and 20 of Act, 1967 (UAPA) and Sections 4 and 5 of Act, 1908. The Additional Sessions Judge, extended the period of completion of investigation. A final report under Section 173(2) of the Code of Criminal Procedure was prepared by the investigating agency and presented before the Court of the Sub- Divisional Judicial Magistrate. The NIA, re-registered the instant case under Sections 17, 18, 18B and 20 of UAPA. The Special Judge, NIA received the entire file from the Court of Additional Sessions Judge, Amritsar. In this manner, the prosecution ultimately stood transferred to the Special Court constituted under the NIA/UAPA. The District Magistrate, accorded sanction for prosecution under the 1908 Act. The Special Judge, NIA recorded that the sanction to prosecute the Accused persons for the offences under the 1908 Act had been accorded and the sanction under the UAPA was being awaited. An application for default bail under Section 167(2) of the Code of Criminal Procedure read with Section 43D of the UAPA was filed before the Special Judge NIA, essentially on the ground that although the chargesheet had been filed within the extended period, yet the same could be termed as incomplete because of want of sanction under the UAPA. In such circumstances, the position was as if there was no chargesheet. The Special Court rejected the application filed by the Accused persons seeking default bail on the ground that the chargesheet had already been filed. Thereafter, the Government accorded sanction for prosecution under the UAPA. The Appellants filed appeal before the High Court against the order passed by the Special Court rejecting the default bail application. A supplementary chargesheet was filed by the NIA before the Special Judge, along with the relevant sanctions for prosecution. The High Court dismissed the appeal filed by the Appellants against the order of the Special Court rejecting the plea of default bail.

Held, while dismissing the appeal:

(i) There was no merit in the principal argument canvassed on behalf of the Appellants that a chargesheet filed without sanction was an incomplete chargesheet which could be termed as not in consonance with Sub-section (5) of Section 173 of the Code of Criminal Procedure. It was conceded by the Appellants that the chargesheet was filed well within the statutory time period i.e., one hundred eighty days, however, the court concerned could not have taken cognizance of such chargesheet in the absence of the orders of sanction not being a part of such chargesheet. Whether the sanction was required or not under a statute, was a question that had to be considered at the time of taking cognizance of the offence and not during inquiry or investigation. There was a marked distinction in the stage of investigation and prosecution. The prosecution starts when the cognizance of offence is taken. It was also to be kept in mind that cognizance was taken of the offence and not of the offender. It could not be said that obtaining sanction from the competent authorities or the authorities concerned was part of investigation. Sanction is required only to enable the court to take cognizance of the offence. The court may take cognizance of the offence after the sanction order was produced before the court, but the moment, the final report was filed along with the documents that may be relied on by the prosecution, then the investigation would be deemed to have been completed. Taking cognizance is entirely different from completing the investigation. To complete the investigation and file a final report was a duty of the investigating agency, but taking cognizance of the offence is the power of the court. The court in a given case, may not take cognizance of the offence for a particular period of time even after filing of the final report. In such circumstance, the Accused concerned could not claim their indefeasible right under Section 167(2) of the Code of Criminal Procedure for being released on default bail. What was contemplated under Section 167(2) of the Code of Criminal Procedure was that the Magistrate or designated Court had no powers to order detention of the Accused beyond the period of one hundred eighty days or ninety days or sixty days as the case may be. If the investigation was concluded within the prescribed period, no right accrues to the Accused concerned to be released on bail under the proviso to Section 167(2) of the Code of Criminal Procedure. [43]

(ii) Once a final report had been filed with all the documents on which the prosecution proposes to rely, the investigation shall be deemed to have been completed. After completing investigation and submitting a final report to the Court, the investigating officer can send a copy of the final report along with the evidence collected and other materials to the sanctioning authority to enable the sanctioning authority to apply his mind to accord sanction. According sanction was the duty of the sanctioning authority who is not connected with the investigation at all. In case the sanctioning authority takes some time to accord sanction, that did not vitiate the final report filed by the investigating agency before the Court. Section 173 of the Code of Criminal Procedure does not speak about the sanction order at all. Section 167 of the Code of Criminal Procedure also speaks only about investigation and not about cognizance by the Magistrate. Therefore, once a final report had been filed, that was the proof of completion of investigation and if final report was filed within the period of one hundred eighty days or ninety days or sixty days from the initial date of remand of Accused concerned, he could not claim that a right had accrued to him to be released on bail for want of filing of sanction order. [44]

(iii) Filing of a chargesheet was sufficient compliance with the provisions of Section 167 of the Code of Criminal Procedure and that an Accused could not claim any indefeasible right of being released on statutory/default bail under Section 167(2) of the Code of Criminal Procedure on the ground that cognizance had not been taken before the expiry of the statutory time period to file the chargesheet. Thiscourt reiterate what this Court said in Suresh Kumar Bhikamchand Jain that grant of sanction was nowhere contemplated under Section 167 of the Code of Criminal Procedure. [63]

(iv) The error on the part of the investigating agency in filing chargesheet first before the Court of Magistrate had nothing to do with the right of the Accused to seek statutory/default bail under Section 167(2) of the Code of Criminal Procedure. The committal proceedings were not warranted, when it comes to prosecution under the UAPA by the NIA by virtue of Section 16 of the NIA Act. This was because the Special Court acts, as one of the original jurisdictions. By virtue of Section 16 of the NIA Act, the Court need not follow the requirements of Section 193 of the Code of Criminal Procedure. [73]

Ratio Decidendi:

Once a final report has been filed, that is the proof of completion of investigation and if final report is filed within the period of one hundred eighty days or ninety days or sixty days from the initial date of remand of Accused, he cannot claim that a right has accrued to him to be released on bail for want of filing of sanction order.

Disposition: In Favour of State.

• • •

CHAPTER VII

Jitendra Kumar Rode vs. Union of India (UOI) (24.04.2023 – SC) : MANU/SC/0450/2023

Relative Section:

Code of Criminal Procedure, 1898 (CrPC) - Section 385, Code of Criminal Procedure, 1898 (CrPC) - Section 423, Code of Criminal Procedure, 1898 (CrPC) - Section 423(1); Code of Criminal Procedure, 1973 (CrPC) - Section 161, Code of Criminal Procedure, 1973 (CrPC) - Section 313, Code of Criminal Procedure, 1973 (CrPC) - Section 377, Code of Criminal Procedure, 1973 (CrPC) - Section 378, Code of Criminal Procedure, 1973 (CrPC) - Section 385, Code of Criminal Procedure, 1973 (CrPC) - Section 386; Constitution of India - Article 21; Indian Penal Code, 1860 (IPC) - Section 302; Prevention Of Corruption Act, 1988 - Section 7, Prevention Of Corruption Act, 1988 - Section 13(1), Prevention Of Corruption Act, 1988 - Section 13(2)

Hon'ble Judges/Coram: Krishna Murari and Sanjay Karol, JJ.

Equivalent Citation: 2023(246)AIC253, 2023 (124) ACC 300, 2023/INSC/605, 2023(2)J.L.J.R.326, 2023 (2)PLJR336, 2023(2)RCR(Criminal)752 I

Number of Pages in the Original Judgment: 11

Case Reference:

V.K. Verma v. CBI MANU/SC/0100/2014; Shyam Deo Pandey and Ors. v. The State of Bihar MANU/SC/0182/1971; State of U.P. v. Abhai Raj Singh and Ors. MANU/SC/0192/2004; Tej Pal Singh and Ors. v. State of U.P. MANU/UP/2283/2015; Madhav Hayawadanrao Hoskot v. State of Maharashtra MANU/SC/0119/1978; Sidhartha Vashisht v. State (NCT of Delhi) MANU/SC/0268/2010; King-Emperor v. Daku Raut MANU/PR/0026/1935; Biswanath Ghosh v. State of West Bengal and Ors. MANU/SC/0208/1987; In Re: Raju Naidu and Ors. MANU/TN/0336/1942; Bani Singh and Ors. v. State of U.P. MANU/SC/0615/1996; Khalil Ahmad v. State of U.P. MANU/UP/0563/1986; Vir Pal and Rama Kant (In Jail) v. State MANU/UP/1502/1999; Hira Lal and Ors. v. State of U.P. MANU/UP/1094/1999; Bhunda and Ors. v. State of U.P. MANU/UP/0863/2001; Ramesh Kaushik v. State of Delhi MANU/DE/4852/2022; Dhananjay Rai alias Guddu Rai v. State of Bihar MANU/SC/0888/2022

Case Note:

Criminal -Absence of record - Validity of conviction - Sections 7, 13(1) and 13(2) of Prevention of Corruption Act, 1988, Sections 313 and 385 of Code of Criminal Procedure, 1973 and Article 21 of Constitution of India - Trial Court convicted Appellant under Sections 7, 13(1) and 13(2) of Act, 1988 - Assailing judgment of conviction and sentence, High Court admitted Petitioner's appeal and despite repeated summoning of records of trial, no reply was received from Court concerned - Record further reveal that entire record had been lost and was not traceable and documents sent as reconstructed documents did not constituterelevant trial court record - High Court, upheld conviction despite having noted on earlier occasion that reconstruction of records was not in accordance with Rules - Hence, present appeal - Whether in absence of records of Court of Trial, appellate Court could have upheld conviction and enhanced quantum of fine and given language employed under Section 385 of Code, present situation constitutes violation of Accused's fundamental rights under Article 21 of Constitution of India.

Facts:

The Trial Court, convicted the Appellant under Sections 7, 13(1) and 13(2) of the Prevention of Corruption Act, 1988. After analysing the evidence on recordthe Trial Court sentenced the Appellant. Assailing the judgment of conviction and sentence, the High Court admitted the Petitioner's appeal and despite repeated summoning of records of the trial, no reply was received from the Court concerned and as a result, the District Judge was asked to furnish an explanation and, in any event, take steps for reconstruction of the record.The record further reveals that the entire record had been lost and was not traceable and the documents sent as reconstructed documents did not constitute the relevant trial court record. The High Court, upheld the conviction despite having noted on an earlier occasion that the reconstruction of records was not in accordance with Rules and the admission of nonavailability of material on record, for which the Appellant was in no manner responsible.

Held, while allowing the appeal:

(i) In the present case, despite efforts, documents such as the witness statements, statements under Section 313 Code of Criminal Procedure were neither available nor have been able to be reconstructed. Therefore, upholding conviction in the absence of such documents could not be said to be in consonance with due process of law and fairness. [19]

(ii) The Court below, by taking a mutually contradictory view, proceeded to decide the appeal on merits sentencing the Accused, forgetting that the challenge was also for conviction. And yet did not deal with the merits of the appeal, laying specific challenge to the judgment of conviction. The whole approach was illegal and erroneous. Firstly, it was observed that the record was missing, and then it casts the onus to produce the same on the Appellant. [32]

(iii) In the facts at hand, the alleged offence in question was committed, and the judgment of the Trial Court was delivered. More than twenty eight years had passed since the commission of the offence. The relevant Trial Court record had not been able to be reconstructed, despite the efforts of the courts below. Hence, ordering a retrial was not in the interest of justice and would not serve any fruitful purpose. The time elapsed must be taken into consideration by the Court, and this court may stress on that, only after taking due note of and taking steps to abide by the warning issued by this Court in Abhai Raj Singh, as was correctly done in Sita Ram. [34]

(iv) Protection of the rights under Article 21 entails protection of liberty from any restriction thereupon in the absence of fair legal procedure. Fair legal procedure includes the opportunity for the person filing an appeal to question the conclusions drawn by the trial court. The same can only be done when the record is available with the Court of Appeal. That is the mandate of Section 385 of the Code of Criminal Procedure. Therefore, it was not within prudence to lay down a straightjacket formula, it was held that non-compliance with the mandate of the section, in certain cases contingent upon specific facts and circumstances of the case, would result in a violation of Article 21 of the Constitution of India, which this court find it to be so in the instant case. [35]

• • •

CHAPTER VIII

Ritu Chhabaria vs. Union of India (UOI) and Ors. (26.04.2023 – SC) : MANU/SC/0459/2023

Relative Section:

Code of Criminal Procedure, 1898 (CrPC) - Section 61, Code of Criminal Procedure, 1898 (CrPC) - Section 167, Code of Criminal Procedure, 1898 (CrPC) - Section 167(2), Code of Criminal Procedure, 1898 (CrPC) - Section 173, Code of Criminal Procedure, 1898 (CrPC) - Section 344; Code of Criminal Procedure, 1973 (CrPC) - Section 154, Code of Criminal Procedure, 1973 (CrPC) - Section 167(2), Code of Criminal Procedure, 1973 (CrPC) - Section 173, Code of Criminal Procedure, 1973 (CrPC) - Section 173(8), Code of Criminal Procedure, 1973 (CrPC) - Section 309, Code of Criminal Procedure, 1973 (CrPC) - Section 309(2); Constitution of India - Article 21, Constitution of India - Article 32, Constitution of India - Article 136, Constitution of India - Article 226; Indian Penal Code, 1860 (IPC) - Section 120(B), Indian Penal Code, 1860 (IPC) - Section 420; Prevention Of Corruption Act, 1988 - Section 7, Prevention Of Corruption Act, 1988 - Section 12, Prevention Of Corruption Act, 1988 - Section 13(1), Prevention Of Corruption Act, 1988 - Section 13(2)

Hon'ble Judges/Coram: Krishna Murari and C.T. Ravikumar, JJ.

Equivalent Citation: 2023(246)AIC81, 2023 (1) ALD(Crl.) 908 (SC), 2023 (124) ACC 647, 2023 (2) ALT (Crl.) 165 (A.P.), 2023(2)CriminalCC474, 2023(385)ELT321(S.C.),2023/INSC/436, 2023(3) J.L.J.R.151, 2023 (2)KLJ794, 2023 (2) MWN (CR.) 1, 2023(3)PLJR31, 2023(3)RCR(Criminal)250, 2023 (2) RLW 1583 (SC)

Number of Pages in the Original Judgment: 12

Case Reference:

M. Ravindran v. The Intelligence Officer, Directorate of Revenue Intelligence MANU/SC/0788/2020; State of Bihar and Ors. v. J.A.C. Saldanha and Ors. MANU/SC/0253/1979; Justice K.S. Puttaswamy and Ors. v. Union of India (UOI) and Ors. MANU/SC/1044/2017; Kavalappara Kottarathil Kochunni Moopil Nayar v. The State of Madras and Ors. MANU/SC/0018/1959; Romesh Thappar v. The State of Madras MANU/SC/0006/1950; Satender Kumar Antil v. Central Bureau of Investigation and Ors.

MANU/SC/1024/2021; Union of India (UOI) and Ors. v. Thamisharasi and Ors. MANU/SC/0714/1995; Ashok Munilal Jain and Ors. v. Assistant Director, Directorate of Enforcement MANU/SC/1846/2017; Dharam Pal v. State of Haryana and Ors. MANU/SC/0118/2016; Ram Narain Popli v. Central Bureau of Investigation MANU/SC/0017/2003; Rajesh Ranjan Yadav v. CBI through its Director MANU/SC/5112/2006

Case Note:

Criminal -Default bail - Supplementary chargesheet - Sections 120(B) and 420 of Code of Criminal Procedure, 1973, Sections 7, 12, 13(1)(d) and 13(2) of Prevention of Corruption Act, 1988 and Sections167(2) and 173(8) of Code of Criminal procedure, 1973 - FIR was lodged under Section 120(B) read with Section 420 of Code along with Sections 7, 12 and 13(2) read with Section 13(1)(d) of Act wherein writ Petitioner's husband was not named - Subsequently, two supplementary chargesheets were filed, wherein writ Petitioner's husband was made prosecution witness in supplementary chargesheet - Investigation was then transferred to another investigating officer, and Accused was then arrested by CBI and was remanded to custody - Multiple other supplementary chargesheets were then filed, wherein Accused was named as suspect, and remand of Accused was renewed and was continued from time to time, and he was never released on default bail - Hence, present petition - Whether chargesheet could be filed in piecemeal without first completing the investigation of case and filing of such chargesheet without completing investigation would extinguish right of Accused for grant of default bail and further remand of Accused could be continued by trial court during pendency of investigation beyond stipulated time as prescribed by Code of Criminal Procedure.

Facts:

An FIR was lodged under Section 120(B) read with Section 420 of the Indian Penal Code, 1860 along with Sections 7, 12 and 13(2) read with Section 13(1)(d) of the Prevention of Corruption Act, 1988, wherein the writ Petitioner's husband was not named.Subsequently, two supplementary chargesheets were filed, wherein the writ Petitioner's husband (Accused) was made a prosecution witness in the supplementary chargesheet. Multiple other supplementary chargesheets were later filed, and the Accused was not named in any of the said chargesheets.The investigation was then transferred to another investigating officer, and the Accused was then arrested by CBI and was remanded to custody. Multiple other supplementary chargesheets were then filed, wherein the Accused herein was named as a suspect, and the remand of the Accused was renewed and was continued from time to time, and he was never released on default bail.The Respondent had admitted in writing in the supplementary chargesheet that the investigation was still pending, and in light of the same the trial court ought not to have issued process and remanded the Petitioner's husband.

Held, while disposing off the petition:

(i) This right of statutory bail, however, is extinguished, if the charge sheet is filed within the stipulated period. The question of resorting to a supplementary chargesheet under Section 173(8) of the Code of Criminal Procedure only arises after the main chargesheet has been filed, and as such, a supplementary chargesheet, wherein it is explicitly stated that the investigation is still pending, cannot under any circumstance, be used to scuttle the right of default bail, for then, the entire purpose of default bail is defeated, and the filing of a chargesheet or a supplementary chargesheet becomes a mere formality, and a tool, to ensure that the right of default bail is scuttled. [24]

(ii) It can be seen that the practice of filing preliminary reports before the enactment of the present Code of Criminal Procedure had now taken the form of filing chargesheets without actually completing the investigation, only to scuttle the right of default bail. If this court were to hold that chargesheets can be filed without completing the investigation, and the same can be used for prolonging remand, it would in effect negate the purpose of introducing Section 167(2) of the Code of Criminal Procedure and ensure that the fundamental rights guaranteed to Accused persons is violated. [27]

(iii) I. Without completing the investigation of a case, a chargesheet or prosecution complaint could not be filed by an investigating agency only to deprive an arrested Accused of his right to default bail under Section 167(2) of the Code of Criminal Procedure.

II. Such a chargesheet, if filed by an investigating authority without first completing the investigation, would not extinguish the right to default bail under Section 167(2) Code of Criminal Procedure.

III. The trial court, in such cases, cannot continue to remand an arrested person beyond the maximum stipulated time without offering the arrested person default bail. [32]

(iv) It was clear from the facts that during the pendency of the investigation, supplementary chargesheets were filed by the Investigation

Agency just before the expiry of sixty days, with the purpose of scuttling the right to default bail accrued in favour the Accused. This factual position was missed by the trial court, and instead of offering default bail to the Accused, the trial court mechanically accepted the incomplete chargesheets filed by the Investigating Agency, and further continued the remand of the Accused beyond the maximum period specified. The Investigating Agency and the trial court, thus, failed to observe the mandate of law, and acted in a manner which was manifestly arbitrary and violative of the fundamental rights guaranteed to the Accused. [33]

Disposition: Disposed of.

• • •

CHAPTER IX

Neeraj Dutta vs. State (Govt. of N.C.T. of Delhi) (15.12.2022 – SC) : MANU/SC/1617/2022

Relative Section:

Code of Criminal Procedure, 1973 (CrPC) - Section 164, Code of Criminal Procedure, 1973 (CrPC) - Section 313; Indian Evidence Act, 1872 - Section 3, Indian Evidence Act, 1872 - Section 4, Indian Evidence Act, 1872 - Section 8, Indian Evidence Act, 1872 - Section 14, Indian Evidence Act, 1872 - Section 59, Indian Evidence Act, 1872 - Section 60, Indian Evidence Act, 1872 - Section 61, Indian Evidence Act, 1872 - Section 62, Indian Evidence Act, 1872 - Section 63, Indian Evidence Act, 1872 - Section 64, Indian Evidence Act, 1872 - Section 65, Indian Evidence Act, 1872 - Section 66, Indian Evidence Act, 1872 - Section 67, Indian Evidence Act, 1872 - Section 67(2), Indian Evidence Act, 1872 - Section 68, Indian Evidence Act, 1872 - Section 69, Indian Evidence Act, 1872 - Section 70, Indian Evidence Act, 1872 - Section 71, Indian Evidence Act, 1872 - Section 72, Indian Evidence Act, 1872 - Section 73, Indian Evidence Act, 1872 - Section 78, Indian Evidence Act, 1872 - Section 79, Indian Evidence Act, 1872 - Section 80, Indian Evidence Act, 1872 - Section 81, Indian Evidence Act, 1872 - Section 83, Indian Evidence Act, 1872 - Section 85, Indian Evidence Act, 1872 - Section 89, Indian Evidence Act, 1872 - Section 105, Indian Evidence Act, 1872 - Section 114, Indian Evidence Act, 1872 - Section 142, Indian Evidence Act, 1872 - Section 154, Indian Evidence Act, 1872 - Section 154(1), Indian Evidence Act, 1872 - Section 154(2); Indian Penal Code, 1860 (IPC) - Section 161, Indian Penal Code, 1860 (IPC) - Section 162, Indian Penal Code, 1860 (IPC) - Section 163, Indian Penal Code, 1860 (IPC) - Section 164, Indian Penal Code, 1860 (IPC) - Section 165, Indian Penal Code, 1860 (IPC) - Section 165A; Negotiable Instruments Act, 1881 - Section 138; Prevention Of Corruption Act, 1947 - Section 4, Prevention Of Corruption Act, 1947 - Section 4(1), Prevention Of Corruption Act, 1947 - Section 5(1), Prevention Of Corruption Act, 1947 - Section 5(2); Prevention Of Corruption Act, 1988 - Section 2, Prevention Of Corruption Act, 1988 - Section 7, Prevention Of Corruption Act, 1988 - Section 11, Prevention Of Corruption Act, 1988 - Section 12, Prevention Of Corruption

Act, 1988 - Section 13, Prevention Of Corruption Act, 1988 - Section 13(1), Prevention Of Corruption Act, 1988 - Section 13(2), Prevention Of Corruption Act, 1988 - Section 14, Prevention Of Corruption Act, 1988 - Section 20, Prevention Of Corruption Act, 1988 - Section 20(1), Prevention Of Corruption Act, 1988 - Section 20(2), Prevention Of Corruption Act, 1988 - Section 31

Hon'ble Judges/Coram:

S. Abdul Nazeer, B.R. Gavai, A.S. Bopanna, V. Ramasubramanian and B.V. Nagarathna, JJ.

Equivalent Citation:

2023(243)AIC70, AIR2023SC330, 2023 (123) ACC 677, 2023(1)BLJ203, 2022(4)Crimes700(SC), 2023(2) Criminal CC425, 295(2022)DLT744, 2022/INSC/1280, 2023(1)J.L.J.R.1, 2022 (7) KHC 647, 2023(2) MLJ (Crl)305, 2023 (1) MWN (CR.) 343, 2023(1)PLJR63, 2023(1)RLW358(SC), (2023)4SCC731, 2023(1)UC104

Number of Pages in the Original Judgment: 32

Case Reference:

P. Satyanarayana Murthy v. The Dist. Inspector of Police and Ors. MANU/SC/1012/2015; Kishan Chand Mangal v. State of Rajasthan MANU/SC/0080/1982; Hazari Lal v. State (Delhi Administration) MANU/SC/0131/1980; M. Narsinga Rao v. State of Andhra Pradesh MANU/SC/0802/2000; B. Jayaraj v. State of A.P. MANU/SC/0245/2014; Subash Parbat Sonvane v. State of Gujarat MANU/SC/0359/2002; Ram Krishan and Ors. v. The State of Delhi MANU/SC/0021/1956; C.K. Damodaran Nair v. Govt of India MANU/SC/0145/1997; A. Subair v. State of Kerala MANU/SC/0890/2009; State of Kerala and Ors. v. C.P. Rao MANU/SC/0678/2011; Suresh Budharmal Kalani v. State of Maharashtra MANU/SC/0608/1998; K. Shanthamma v. State of Karnataka MANU/SC/0218/2022; State of U.P. v. Ram Asrey MANU/SC/0517/1990; Mukhtiar Singh (since deceased) through his L.R. v. State of Punjab MANU/SC/0809/2017; M.R. Purushotham v. State of Karnataka MANU/SC/0868/2014; C.M. Sharma v. State of A.P. Th. I.P. MANU/SC/0981/2010; State of Maharashtra v. Dnyaneshwar Laxman Rao Wankhede MANU/SC/1339/2009; C. Sukumaran v. State of Kerala MANU/SC/0076/2015; N. Sunkanna v. State of Andhra Pradesh MANU/SC/1158/2015; State of Madhya Pradesh and Ors. v. Ram Singh MANU/SC/0064/2000; State of Rajasthan v. Babu Meena MANU/SC/0152/2013; Kumar Exports v. Sharma Carpets MANU/SC/8414/2008; Krishna Janardhan Bhat v. Dattatraya G. Hegde MANU/SC/

0503/2008; The State of Madras v. A. Vaidyanatha Iyer MANU/SC/0108/1957; Dhanvantrai Balwantrai Desai v. State of Maharashtra MANU/SC/0150/1962; Navaneethakrishnan v. The State MANU/SC/0385/2018; Sharad Birdhichand Sarda v. State of Maharashtra MANU/SC/0111/1984; Prakash v. State of Rajasthan MANU/SC/0278/2013; Kundan Lal Rallaram v. Custodian, Evacuee Property, Bombay MANU/SC/0422/1961; Madhukar Bhaskarrao Joshi v. State of Maharashtra MANU/SC/0680/2000; State through Central Bureau of Investigation v. Anup Kumar Srivastava MANU/SC/0955/2017; State of Andhra Pradesh v. V. Vasudeva Rao MANU/SC/0916/2003; State of Andhra Pradesh v. P. Venkateshwarlu MANU/SC/0560/2015; Selvaraj v. State of Karnataka MANU/SC/1004/2015; Nayankumar Shivappa Waghmare v. State of Maharashtra MANU/SC/0158/2015; Prakash Chand v. State (Delhi Administration) MANU/SC/0147/1978; Sat Paul v. Delhi Administration MANU/SC/0203/1975; Baikuntha Nath Chattoraj v. Prasannamoyi Debya and another MANU/PR/0133/1922; Swatantar Singh v. State of Haryana and Ors. MANU/SC/0510/1997; A.B. Bhaskara Rao v. Inspector of Police, CBI, Visakhapatnam MANU/SC/1110/2011; State of Madhya Pradesh v. Shambhu Dayal Nagar MANU/SC/8623/2006; Amarjit Singh v. State (Delhi Admn.) MANU/DE/0891/1994 : 1995 Cr LJ 1623 (Del)

Case Note:

Service - Culpability of public servant -Nature and quality of proof - Section 7 and Section 13(1)(d) read with Section 13(2) of Prevention of Corruption Act, 1988 - Issue is with regard to establishment of demand of illegal gratification for conviction - Whether, in the absence of evidence of complainant/direct or primary evidence of demand of illegal gratification, is it not permissible to draw an inferential deduction of culpability/guilt of a public servant under Section 7 and Section 13(1)(d) read with Section 13(2) of Act, 1988 based on other evidence adduced by the prosecution?

Facts:

The moot question that arises for answering the reference is, in the absence of the complainant letting in direct evidence of demand owing to the non-availability of the complainant or owing to his death or other reason, whether the demand for illegal gratification could be established by other evidence. Two three-judge benches of this Court, in the cases of B. Jayaraj v. State of Andhra Pradesh; and P. Satyanarayana Murthy v. District Inspector of Police, State of Andhra Pradesh and Anr., are in conflict with an earlier three-judge bench decision of this Court in M. Narsinga Rao v.

State of A.P., regarding the nature and quality of proof necessary to sustain a conviction for the offences under Section 7 and 13(1)(d) read with Section 13(2) of the Act, 1988 when the primary evidence of the complainant is unavailable.

Held, while answering the reference

1.Even if a witness is treated as "hostile" and is cross-examined, his evidence cannot be written off altogether but must be considered with due care and circumspection and that part of the testimony which is creditworthy must be considered and acted upon. It is for the judge as a matter of prudence to consider the extent of evidence which is creditworthy for the purpose of proof of the case. In other words, the fact that a witness has been declared "hostile" does not result in an automatic rejection of his evidence. Even, the evidence of a "hostile witness" if it finds corroboration from the facts of the case may be taken into account while judging the guilt of the Accused. Thus, there is no legal bar to raise a conviction upon a "hostile witness" testimony if corroborated by other reliable evidence.[67]

2. Proof of demand and acceptance of illegal gratification by a public servant as a fact in issue by the prosecution is a sine qua non in order to establish the guilt of the Accused public servant Under Sections 7 and 13(1)(d)(i) and (ii) of the Act. In order to bring home the guilt of the Accused, the prosecution has to first prove the demand of illegal gratification and the subsequent acceptance as a matter of fact. This fact in issue can be proved either by direct evidence which can be in the nature of oral evidence or documentary evidence. Further, the fact in issue, namely, the proof of demand and acceptance of illegal gratification can also be proved by circumstantial evidence in the absence of direct oral and documentary evidence. The presumption of fact with regard to the demand and acceptance or obtainment of an illegal gratification may be made by a court of law by way of an inference only when the foundational facts have been proved by relevant oral and documentary evidence and not in the absence thereof. On the basis of the material on record, the Court has the discretion to raise a presumption of fact while considering whether the fact of demand has been proved by the prosecution or not. Of course, a presumption of fact is subject to rebuttal by the Accused and in the absence of rebuttal presumption stands. In the event the complainant turns 'hostile', or has died or is unavailable to let in his evidence during trial, demand of illegal gratification can be proved by letting in the evidence of any other

witness who can again let in evidence, either orally or by documentary evidence or the prosecution can prove the case by circumstantial evidence. The trial does not abate nor does it result in an order of acquittal of the Accused public servant. In so far as Section 7 of the Act is concerned, on the proof of the facts in issue, Section 20 mandates the court to raise a presumption that the illegal gratification was for the purpose of a motive or reward as mentioned in the said Section. The said presumption has to be raised by the court as a legal presumption or a presumption in law. Said presumption is also subject to rebuttal. Section 20 does not apply to Section 13(1)(d)(i) and (ii) of the Act. The presumption in law under Section 20 of the Act is distinct from presumption of fact referred to above as the former is a mandatory presumption while the latter is discretionary in nature. [68]

3. There is no conflict in the three judge Bench decisions of this Court in B. Jayaraj and P. Satyanarayana Murthy with the three judge Bench decision in M. Narasinga Rao, with regard to the nature and quality of proof necessary to sustain a conviction for offences Under Sections 7 or 13(1)(d)(i) and (ii) of the Act, when the direct evidence of the complainant or "primary evidence" of the complainant is unavailable owing to his death or any other reason. The position of law when a complainant or prosecution witness turns "hostile" is also discussed and the observations made above would accordingly apply in light of Section 154 of the Evidence Act. There is no conflict between the judgments in the aforesaid three cases. [69]

4. Accordingly, the question referred for consideration of this Constitution Bench is answered that, in the absence of evidence of the complainant (direct/primary, oral/documentary evidence), it is permissible to draw an inferential deduction of culpability/guilt of a public servant under Section 7 and Section 13(1)(d) read with Section 13(2) of the Act based on other evidence adduced by the prosecution. [70]

Ratio Decidendi: There is no legal bar to raise a conviction upon a "hostile witness" testimony if corroborated by other reliable evidence.

• • •

CHAPTER X

T.P. Gopalakrishnan vs. State of Kerala (08.12.2022 – SC) : MANU /SC/1654/2022

Relative Section:

Code of Criminal Procedure, 1973 (CrPC) - Section 188, Code of Criminal Procedure, 1973 (CrPC) - Section 197(1), Code of Criminal Procedure, 1973 (CrPC) - Section 220(1), Code of Criminal Procedure, 1973 (CrPC) - Section 221(1), Code of Criminal Procedure, 1973 (CrPC) - Section 258, Code of Criminal Procedure, 1973 (CrPC) - Section 300, Code of Criminal Procedure, 1973 (CrPC) - Section 300(1), Code of Criminal Procedure, 1973 (CrPC) - Section 300(2), Code of Criminal Procedure, 1973 (CrPC) - Section 300(3), Code of Criminal Procedure, 1973 (CrPC) - Section 300(4), Code of Criminal Procedure, 1973 (CrPC) - Section 300(5), Code of Criminal Procedure, 1973 (CrPC) - Section 313; Constitution of India - Article 20, Constitution of India - Article 20(2), Constitution of India - Article 21, Constitution of India - Article 22; General Clauses Act 1897 - Section 26; Indian Evidence Act, 1872 - Section 40; Indian Penal Code, 1860 (IPC) - Section 71, Indian Penal Code, 1860 (IPC) - Section 409, Indian Penal Code, 1860 (IPC) - Section 477A; Prevention Of Corruption Act, 1988 - Section 13(1), Prevention Of Corruption Act, 1988 - Section 13(2), Prevention Of Corruption Act, 1988 - Section 19

Hon'ble Judges/Coram: B.R. Gavai and B.V. Nagarathna, JJ.

Equivalent Citation: 2023(242)AIC61, 2023 (122) ACC 946, 2023ALLMR(Cri)748, 2023CriLJ1153, 2023(1)CriminalCC175, 2023(1)CTC230, 2022/INSC/1262, 2023(1)J.L.J.R.359, 2023(1)JLJ335, 2023(1)KLT397, 2023(2)N.C.C.238, 2023(1)PLJR427

Number of Pages in the Original Judgment: 15

Case Reference:

Thakur Ram v. The State of Bihar MANU/SC/0094/1965; S.A. Venkataraman v. The Union of India (UOI) and Ors. MANU/SC/0133/1954; Maqbool Hussain v. The State of Bombay MANU/SC/0062/1953; State (N.C.T. of Delhi) v. Navjot Sandhu and Ors. MANU/SC/0465/2005; Vijayalakshmi v. Vasudevan (1994) 4 SCC 656; Maneka Gandhi v. Union of India MANU/SC/0133/1978 : 1978 AIR 597

Case Note:

Criminal -Conviction - Legality - Section 13(2) read with Section 13(1)(c) of the Prevention of Corruption Act, 1988 and Section 409 of the Indian Penal Code, 1860 ('IPC') and Section 300 of the Code of Criminal Procedure, 1973 (CrPC) - Present Appeals have been filed assailing the impugned judgment passed by the High Court by which the judgment of conviction and order of sentence passed by the Trial Court has been upheld by dismissing the appeals and consequently confirming the conviction of the Appellant - Whether the High Court was justified in confirming the judgment of conviction and sentence of Trial Court?

Facts:

The Trial Court vide its judgment and order convicted the Appellant herein-Accused for offences under Section 13(2) read with Section 13(1)(c) of the Act, 1988 and sentenced him to undergo rigorous imprisonment for two years and to pay a fine of Rupees Two Thousand and in default thereof, to undergo rigorous imprisonment for six months. The Accused was further convicted for the offence Under Section 409 of the IPC and sentenced to undergo rigorous imprisonment for two years and to pay a fine of Rupees Two Thousand and in default thereof, to undergo rigorous imprisonment for six months. The sentences were directed to run concurrently. Present Appeals have been filed assailing the impugned judgment passed by the High Court by which the judgment of conviction and order of sentence passed by the Trial Court has been upheld.

Held, while allowing the appeal

1. The Trial Court has erred in holding that the facts of previous case and misappropriation committed by the Accused are not the same as the facts relevant to present case. The Trial Court has held that in the present case, the allegation is that after conducting the auction of coconuts and half filled grains, two-thirds of the amount collected from the successful bidder was not remitted to the treasury, however, in the earlier cases, the allegations were that the Accused misappropriated some amount to be paid to the proprietor of Agricultural Marketing Corporation, Kozhikode, Kerala State Coir marketing Corporation, Kozhikode from the State Seed Farm, Perambra by forging and falsifying records. It is the admitted case of the prosecution that the present cases were based on the re-audit conducted by PW-9-the Assistant Sub-Inspector, Vigilance and Anti-Corruption Bureau, Kozhikode. The re-audit was done for the period from 01.04.1992 to 31.12.1994. The charges in the present case are for relevant period from

27.04.1992 to 25.08.1992 and 01.03.1993 to 12.04.1994 which time period is same as in the previous three cases, that is, 28.03.1994 to 02.04.1994, 15.12.1992 to 31.03.1993 and 05.03.1994 to 08.03.1994 respectively. Thus, it can be said that the present cases pertain to the same set of facts and are in respect of same offences, for the same period, committed in the same capacity as the previous three cases wherein the Appellant herein was already prosecuted in the year 1999. The core allegation in all these five cases pertains to misappropriation by making false entries in the cash book. The allegation of the prosecution that two-thirds of the auction amount was not remitted to the treasury would be covered under the allegations of misappropriation of funds, that the Appellant has already been prosecuted for in the year 1999. The Appellant is right in contending that the charge in the first three cases were framed on 17.08.1999 which is much after the audit and the prosecution would have been well aware of the misappropriation in respect of the present cases on 17.08.1999. [38]

2. The allegations/offences in the instant cases are the same as the allegations/offences in the previous three cases, therefore as per the mandate Under Section 300(2) of the Code of Criminal Procedure, the consent of the State Government is necessary. Even if it is assumed for the sake of argument that the allegations are different in present cases from those in the previous cases, the prosecution has failed to obtain the prior consent of the State Government necessary to prosecute the Accused-Appellant and therefore the trial in the instant case is unlawful. [39]

3. It would not be wrong to say that the charges framed against the Accused reveal that there were several acts of misappropriation and falsification of accounts however the same were committed in the same transaction as the one for which he was prosecuted in the year 1999. The series of acts alleged against him are so connected to one another. [40]

4. Sub-section (2) of Section 300 of the CrPC states that when the charge of the second trial is for a distinct offence, the trial is not barred. This means that if a person is acquitted or convicted of any offence, he may be tried for a distinct offence for which a separate charge might have been made against him at the former trial Under Sub-section (1) of Section 220 of the Code of Criminal Procedure but the same is subject to a condition precedent being, that the consent of the State Government is sought before such a person could be tried. Earlier the Petitioner was tried in C.C. No. 12 of 1999, C.C. No. 13 of 1999 and C.C. No. 14 of 1999 for the offences Under Section 13(1)(c) read with Section 13(2) of the Act as well as Under

Sections 409 and 477A of the Indian Penal Code. In C.C. No. 24 of 2003 and C.C. No. 25 of 2003, the Appellant is being tried once again for the offences Under Section 13(1)(c) read with Section 13(2) of the Act and Section 409 of the IPC for the same period. There is no material on record to demonstrate that C.C. No. 24 of 2003 and C.C. No. 25 of 2003 have been initiated pursuant to the consent of the State Government. It is also not brought on record that the C.C. No. 24 of 2003 and C.C. No. 25 of 2003 is for any distinct offence for which a separate charge had been made against the Appellant and the earlier trials. Having re-appreciated the evidence of the witnesses and on considering the contentions of the rival parties, we find that the High Court was not justified in affirming the judgment of conviction and sentence passed by the Trial Court. e Trial Court as well as the High Court were not right in convicting and sentencing the Appellant herein and therefore, the impugned judgments are liable to be set aside. [41]

5. Appeals allowed. [42]

Disposition: In Favour of Accused.

• • •

CHAPTER XI

The State of Chhattisgarh and Ors. vs. Aman Kumar Singh and Ors. (01.03.2023 – SC) : MANU /SC/0184/2023

Relative Section:

Chhattisgarh Civil Services (Conduct) Rules, 1965; Code of Criminal Procedure, 1973 (CrPC) - Section 156, Code of Criminal Procedure, 1973 (CrPC) - Section 173(2), Code of Criminal Procedure, 1973 (CrPC) - Section 482; Constitution of India - Article 21, Constitution of India - Article 226; Indian Penal Code, 1860 (IPC) - Section 120(B), Indian Penal Code, 1860 (IPC) - Section 120B, Indian Penal Code, 1860 (IPC) - Section 211; Prevention of Corruption (Amendment) Act, 2018; Prevention Of Corruption Act, 1988 - Section 2(c), Prevention Of Corruption Act, 1988 - Section 13, Prevention Of Corruption Act, 1988 - Section 13(1), Prevention Of Corruption Act, 1988 - Section 13(2)

Hon'ble Judges/Coram: S. Ravindra Bhat and Dipankar Datta, JJ.

Equivalent Citation: AIR2023SC1441, 2023/INSC/189, 2023(2)MLJ(Crl)105, 2023(2)RCR (Criminal) 124, (2023)6SCC559, 2023(2)UC1050

Number of Pages in the Original Judgment: 18

Case Reference: Superintendent of Police, C.B.I. and Ors. v. Tapan Kr. Singh MANU/SC/0299/2003; State of U.P. v. Naresh and Ors. MANU/SC/0228/2011; Neeharika Infrastructure Pvt. Ltd. v. State of Maharashtra and Ors. MANU/SC/0272/2021; Central Bureau of Investigation and Ors. v. Thommandru Hannah Vijayalakshmi and Ors. MANU/SC/0831/2021; R.P. Kapur v. The State of Punjab MANU/SC/0086/1960; State of Haryana and Ors. v. Ch. Bhajan Lal and Ors. MANU/SC/0115/1992; Rajesh Bajaj v. State NCT of Delhi and Ors. MANU/SC/0155/1999; Lalita Kumari v. Govt. of U.P. and Ors. MANU/SC/1166/2013; State of Maharashtra and Ors. v. Ishwar Piraji Kalpatri and Ors. MANU/SC/0194/1996; State of Bihar and Ors. v. P.P. Sharma and Ors. MANU/SC/0542/1992; Directorate of Enforcement v. Anil Tuteja and Ors. W.P. (Crl.) No. 506 of 2021

Case Note:

Criminal - Quashing of FIR - Maintainability thereof - Complaint was lodged in office of Chief Minister of State alleged therein that Respondent, his wife and his family were involved in corruption and money laundering, and that he also held assets which are disproportionate to his known sources of income - Complaint enquired into by Economic Offences Wing and FIR was registered against Respondents - Writ petition was filed by Respondents for quashing of FIR - High Court quashed FIR registered against Respondents - Hence, present appeal - Whether High Court erred in quashing FIR registered against Respondents.

Facts:

A complaint was lodged in the office of the Chief Minister of the State. It was alleged therein that Respondent-Indian Revenue Service (IRS) officer and the former Principal Secretary to the erstwhile Chief Minister of Chhattisgarh, his wife and his family were involved in corruption and money laundering, and that he also held assets which are disproportionate to his known sources of income.Upon the complaint being received, the Chief Minister by a handwritten order directed the Chief Secretary of the State to have the complaint enquired into by the Economic Offences Wing (EOW) and FIR was registered against Respondents. The High Court quashed FIR registered against Respondents.

Held, while allowing the appeal:

(i) It was found on perusal of the FIR that although not specifically mentioned, was the check period during which Respondents had acquired property disproportionate to their known sources of income. There were certain calculations projecting the quantum of money that both Respondents received towards salaries, interest and value for properties sold. Particulars of immovable properties acquired by Respondents at different locations with particulars of price also find mention therein. It was thereafter stated that in addition to these properties, there is possibility of there being other properties in other places of the country in the names of Respondents. There were also references to possible investments made by Respondent abroad, either in his own name or in the names of his wife and dependent members. Deposits of money in lakhs in the bank account of Respondent regularly had been suspected to be receipt of consideration (profit) from investment of big amounts. It was also revealed from the FIR that sum were deposited in the bank account of Respondent and such financial transactions involving huge amounts prima facie appeared to be conspicuous requiring minute scrutiny. [55]

(ii) The pleadings were insufficient to return a finding that the FIR was an outcome of mala fide. No doubt, certain allegations were levelled against the Government and the Chief Minister, however, such allegations are vague and general in nature. Mala fide motives were required to be affirmatively pleaded and proved. However, no foundation in that behalf had been laid and naturally so, the High Court even did not examine whether exception could have been taken to the FIR on the ground of mala fide.[71]

(iii) There were no cogent grounds for quashing the FIR in the present case even on the ground of mala fide. [75]

Disposition: In Favour of Accused.

• • •

CHAPTER XII

Neeraj Dutta vs. State (Govt. of N.C.T. of Delhi) (17.03.2023 – SC) : MANU/SC/0250/2023

Relative Section:

Code of Criminal Procedure, 1973 (CrPC) - Section 313; Prevention Of Corruption Act, 1988 - Section 2, Prevention Of Corruption Act, 1988 - Section 7, Prevention Of Corruption Act, 1988 - Section 12, Prevention Of Corruption Act, 1988 - Section 13, Prevention Of Corruption Act, 1988 - Section 13(1), Prevention Of Corruption Act, 1988 - Section 13(2), Prevention Of Corruption Act, 1988 - Section 20

Hon'ble Judges/Coram: Abhay Shreeniwas Oka and Rajesh Bindal, JJ.

Equivalent Citation: 2023(245)AIC172, 2023 (124) ACC 697, 2023CriLJ1856, 2023(2) Crimes 78 (SC) ,299(2023)DLT131, 2023/INSC/245, 2023(2)N.C.C.443, 2023(I)OLR688, 2023(2)RCR (Criminal) 762, [2023] 2SCR997, 2023(2)ShimLC721

Number of Pages in the Original Judgment: 12

Case Reference:

B. Jayaraj v. State of A.P. MANU/SC/0245/2014; P. Satyanarayana Murthy v. The Dist. Inspector of Police and Ors. MANU/SC/1012/2015; M. Narsinga Rao v. State of Andhra Pradesh MANU/SC/0802/2000; N. Vijayakumar v. State of Tamil Nadu MANU/SC/0051/2021; C.M. Girish Babu v. CBI, Cochin, High Court of Kerala MANU/SC/0274/2009; Neeraj Dutta v. State (Govt. of N.C.T. of Delhi) MANU/SC/1617/2022

Case Note:

Criminal - Acquittal - Illegal gratification - Sections 7, 12, 13(1)(d)(i), 13(1)(d)(ii) and 13(2) of Prevention of Corruption Act, 1988 - Appellant was convicted by Special Judge for offence of illegal gratification punishable under Section 7 and Clauses (i) and (ii) of Section 13(1)(d) read with Section 13(2) of Act - Co-Accused was convicted for offence punishable under Section 12 of Act -Special Court held that there was sufficient circumstantial evidence on record to prove guilt of Appellant - In appeal, conviction of Appellant had been upheld by High Court, however co-Accused was acquitted by High Court - Hence, present appeal - Whether on basis of evidence on record, prosecution had proved demand of gratification by Accused.

Facts:

The Appellant was convicted by the Special Judge for the offence of illegal gratification punishable under Section 7 and Clauses (i) and (ii) of Section 13(1)(d) read with Section 13(2) of the Prevention of Corruption Act, 1988. The co-Accused, was convicted by the Special Judge for the offence punishable Under Section 12 of the PC Act. The Special Court held that there was sufficient circumstantial evidence on record to prove the guilt of the Appellant. In fact, a finding was recorded on the basis of circumstantial evidence that the demand and acceptance were proved. The order of conviction of the Special Court as regards the Appellant has been confirmed by the High Court in the impugned judgment, however the co-Accused was acquitted by the High Court.

Held, while allowing the appeal:

(i) When this court consider the issue of proof of demand within the meaning of Section 7, it could not be a simpliciter demand for money but it has to be a demand of gratification other than legal remuneration. All that prosecution witness say was when the Appellant visited the shop of the complainant, she asked the complainant to give papers regarding the electricity meter and money to her by telling him that she was in a hurry. This was not a case where a specific demand of gratification for providing electricity meter was made by the Appellant to the complainant in the presence of the shadow witness. Prosecution witness had not stated that there was any discussion in his presence between the Appellant and the complainant on the basis of which an inference could have been drawn that there was a demand made for gratification by the Appellant. The witness had no knowledge about what transpired between the complainant and the Appellant earlier. Prosecution witness had admittedly no personal knowledge about the purpose for which the cash was allegedly handed over by the complainant to the Appellant. [16]

(ii) As per the version of the Appellant in her statement, she was working as an LDC. On that day, she was busy with her official duty in a collection drive organized by the department to collect dues from the consumers. Her explanation was that the complainant was her neighbour and he wanted her assistance to deposit electricity charges. She stated that earlier, she had a transaction of sale and purchase of a car through the complainant. She had also stated that the complainant was a history-sheeter and there were three First Information Reports (FIRs) registered against him. In this context, Prosecution witness was questioned in the cross-examination. It was pertinent to note here that prosecution witness did not confirm the correctness of the suggestion but stated that he was not in a position to deny the same. In fact, another prosecution witness, the investigation officer, deposed that cash was found in the Appellant's car. This lends support to the defence that there was a recovery drive conducted by the Appellant. Apart from the evidence of prosecution witness, there was no other evidence that was pressed into service by the prosecution for proving the demand by the Appellant. Even taking the statements of prosecution witness in the examination-in-chief as correct, it was impossible to even infer that the demand of money was made by the Appellant by way of gratification. Every demand made for payment of money was not a demand for gratification. It had to be something more than mere demand for money. [17]

(iii) In the present case, there were no circumstances brought on record which would prove the demand for gratification. Therefore, the ingredients of the offence under Section 7 of the PC Act were not established and consequently, the offence under Section 13(1)(d) would not be attracted. [19]

Disposition: In Favour of Accused.

• • •

CHAPTER XIII

Central Bureau of Investigation vs. Santosh Karnani and Ors.(17.04.2023-SC):MANU/SC/0384/2023

Relative Section:

Code of Criminal Procedure, 1973 (CrPC) - Section 41A, Code of Criminal Procedure, 1973 (CrPC) - Section 438; Constitution of India - Article 21; Income-tax Act, 1961 - Section 133A; Indian Penal Code, 1860 (IPC) - Section 34, Indian Penal Code, 1860 (IPC) - Section 149; Prevention Of Corruption Act, 1988 - Section 7, Prevention Of Corruption Act, 1988 - Section 13(1), Prevention Of Corruption Act, 1988 - Section 13(2), Prevention Of Corruption Act, 1988 - Section 17A

Hon'ble Judges/Coram: Surya Kant and J.K. Maheshwari, JJ.

Equivalent Citation: 2023(2)Crimes330(SC), 2023/INSC/380, 2023(3)RCR(Criminal)213

Number of Pages in the Original Judgment: 13

Case Reference:

D.K. Basu v. State of West Bengal MANU/SC/0157/1997; State Rep. by the C.B.I. v. Anil Sharma MANU/SC/0947/1997; Prem Shankar Prasad v. The State of Bihar and Ors. MANU/SC/0951/2021; State of Madhya Pradesh v. Pradeep Sharma MANU/SC/1262/2013; Lavesh v. State (NCT of Delhi) MANU/SC/0701/2012; Arnesh Kumar v. State of Bihar MANU/SC/0559/2014; Dolat Ram and Ors. v. State of Haryana MANU/SC/0547/1995; Siddharam Satlingappa Mhetre v. State of Maharashtra and Ors. MANU/SC/1021/2010; Gurbaksh Singh Sibbia and Ors. v. State of Punjab MANU/SC/0215/1980; Sushila Aggarwal v. State (NCT of Delhi) MANU/SC/0100/2020

Case Note:

Criminal -Anticipatory bail -Cancellation of - Sections 7, 13(1),13(2) and 17A of Prevention of Corruption Act, 1988 - FIR was registered against Respondent No. 1 for offence of illegal gratification under Sections 7, 13(1) and 13(2) of Act and case was transferred to CBI - Respondent No.1 preferred application for grant of anticipatory bail - City Civil & Sessions Court rejected Respondent No. 1's application for anticipatory bail - Special

Court held that custodial interrogation of Respondent No. 1 was necessary to reach root of matter - Aggrieved by order of Special Judge, Respondent No. 1 applied for anticipatory bail before High Court - High Court, granted anticipatory bail to Respondent No. 1 by observing that there was doubt regarding acceptance of illegal gratification and there was no evidence with respect to acceptance of amount by Respondent No. 1 - Hence, present appeal - Whether High Court erred in granting anticipatory bail to Respondent No.1.

Facts:

FIR was registered against Respondent No. 1 under Sections 7, 13(1) and 13(2) of the Prevention of Corruption Act, 1988. Notice was issued to Respondent No. 1 to participate in investigation and he failed to appear before the CBI. He simultaneously preferred an application for grant of anticipatory bail. The City Civil & Sessions Court rejected Respondent No. 1's application for anticipatory bail. The Special Judge observed thatRespondent No. 1 instead of cooperating with the investigating agency, had absconded and got himself admitted in ahospital to evade the process of law.The Court eventually held that custodial interrogation of Respondent No. 1 was necessary to reach the root of the matter.Aggrieved by the order of the Special Judge, CBI Court, Respondent No. 1 applied for anticipatory bail before the High Court. The High Court, vide impugned order granted anti-cipatory bail to Respondent No. 1. The High Court observed that there was a doubt regarding the acceptance of illegal gratification, and there was no evidence with respect to acceptance of the amount by Respondent No. 1.

Held, while allowing the appeal:

(i) The manner in which Respondent No. 1 forcefully evaded his arrest with the help of his colleagues and got the evidence destroyed, was a strong circumstance to indicate his complicity at this stage though a clear picture would emerge only on completion of investigation. [30]

(ii) From the material placed on record, it seems that prima facie, the allegations against Respondent No. 1 could not be brushed aside lightly at this stage. There appears to be a well-organised syndicate comprising officers and officials of the Income Tax Department, businessmen and Hawala traders, who were in tandem. Such a nexus needs to be unearthed through an unimpaired and unobstructed investigation. [32]

(iii) The contention that prior approval of investigation, as mandated under Section 17A of Prevention of Corruption Act, had not been obtained and thus, the proceedings initiated against Respondent No. 1 stand vitiated, had no legal or factual basis. Section 17A merely contemplates that police officers shall not conduct any enquiry, inquiry or investigation into any offence alleged to have been committed by a public servant where the alleged offence was relatable to any recommendation made or decision taken in discharge of official functions or duties, without the previous approval of the competent authority. The first proviso to the Section states that such approval was not necessary in cases involving arrest of the person on the spot on the charges of accepting undue advantage. [33]

Disposition: In Favour of State.

• • •

CHAPTER XIV

Jagtar Singh vs. State of Punjab (23.03.2023 – SC) : MANU /SC/0288/2023

Relative Section:

Code of Criminal Procedure, 1973 (CrPC) - Section 313; Prevention Of Corruption Act, 1988 - Section 7, Prevention Of Corruption Act, 1988 - Section 13(1), Prevention Of Corruption Act, 1988 - Section 13(2), Prevention Of Corruption Act, 1988 - Section 20

Hon'ble Judges/Coram: Abhay Shreeniwas Oka and Rajesh Bindal, JJ.

Equivalent Citation: 2023(245)AIC117, AIR2023SC1567, 2023(123)ACC938, 2023(2)Crimes14(SC), 2023 (2)CriminalCC607, 2023/INSC/279, 2023(1)MWN(CR.)573, 2023(2)RCR(Criminal)499, 2023 (2)ShimLC781

Number of Pages in the Original Judgment: 5

Case Reference: Neeraj Dutta v. State (Govt. of NCT of Delhi) MANU/ SC/1617/2022

Case Note:

Criminal - Acquittal - Illegal gratification - Appellant was convicted by Trial Court for offence of illegal gratification in respect of getting of death certificate - In appeal, conviction of appellant was upheld by High Court - Hence, present appeal - Whether impugned judgment of conviction warrant any interference.

Facts:

In the complaint, it was alleged that for getting the death certificate of deceased, his son, requested complainant to collect the same. The complainant met the Appellant in connection with supply of death certificate, who demanded illegal gratification. FIR was registered and charge sheet was filed against Appellant. Thereafter, Appellant was convicted by Trial Court for offence of illegal gratification and same was upheld by the High Court.

Held, while allowing the appeal:

(i) In the case in hand, shadow witness had turned hostile. The Trial Court had specifically held that there was no evidence produced on record to prove the demand of illegal gratification. It was not the case in which the demand was reiterated when the money was allegedly paid to him. District Social Security Officer was only a witness who stated that he had recovered the money from the Appellant. The High Court had passed its judgment on the assumption that the money having been recovered from the Appellant, there was demand of illegal gratification. This was not a case where there was circumstantial evidence to prove the demand. [11]

Disposition: Appeal Allowed.

• • •

CHAPTER XV

Anoop Bartaria and Ors. vs. Dy. Director Enforcement Directorate and Ors. (21.04.2023 – SC) : MANU/SC/0438/2023

Relative Section:

Code of Criminal Procedure, 1973 (CrPC) - Section 155(2), Code of Criminal Procedure, 1973 (CrPC) - Section 156(1), Code of Criminal Procedure, 1973 (CrPC) - Section 482; Companies Act, 1956; Constitution of India - Article 226; Finance (No. 2) Act, 2019; Indian Penal Code, 1860 (IPC) - Section 120B, Indian Penal Code, 1860 (IPC) - Section 420, Indian Penal Code, 1860 (IPC) - Section 467, Indian Penal Code, 1860 (IPC) - Section 468, Indian Penal Code, 1860 (IPC) - Section 471, Indian Penal Code, 1860 (IPC) - Section 472, Indian Penal Code, 1860 (IPC) - Section 474; Prevention Of Corruption Act, 1988 - Section 13(1), Prevention Of Corruption Act, 1988 - Section 13(2); Prevention of Money-Laundering (Amendment) Act, 2005; Prevention Of Money-laundering Act, 2002 - Section 2(u), Prevention Of Money-laundering Act, 2002 - Section 2(y), Prevention Of Money-laundering Act, 2002 - Section 2(1), Prevention Of Money-laundering Act, 2002 - Section 3, Prevention Of Money-laundering Act, 2002 - Section 4, Prevention Of Money-laundering Act, 2002 - Section 19, Prevention Of Money-laundering Act, 2002 - Section 45, Prevention Of Money-laundering Act, 2002 - Section 45(1)

Hon'ble Judges/Coram: Ajay Rastogi and Bela M. Trivedi, JJ.

Equivalent Citation:2023(246) AIC229,2023/INSC/413, 2023(3)MLJ(Crl)434,2023(3)RCR (Criminal) 617,2023(3)RLW2566(SC), [2023]178SCL465(SC)

Number of Pages in the Original Judgment: 10

Case Reference:

Nikesh Tarachand Shah v. Union of India (UOI) and Ors. MANU/SC/ 1480/2017; Pepsi Foods Ltd. and Ors. v. Special Judicial Magistrate and Ors. MANU/SC/1090/1998; State of Haryana and Ors. v. Ch. Bhajan Lal and Ors. MANU/SC/0115/1992

Case Note:

Criminal - Quashing of proceedings - Denial of - Sections 120B, 420, 467, 468, 471, 472 and 474 of Indian Penal Code, 1860, Sections 13(1)(d) and 13(2) of Prevention of Corruption Act, 1988and Sections 2(u), 2(y) and 3 of Prevention of Money Laundering Act, 2002 - FIR was registered by CBI against one person, his associates and officials of three branches of bank and certain other persons for offences under Sections 120B, 420, 467, 468, 471, 472 and 474 of Code and Section 13(2) read with 13(1)(d) of Act - It was alleged in said FIR that to defraud bank, Accused and his associates, in collusion with officials of bank had misused KYC documents of his clients/employees/family members as well as existing customers of bank -During course of investigation, it was revealed that Petitioner, his companies had received more than one hundred sixty crores defrauded funds from accounts of fictitious firms/companies - Petitioner therefore filed writ petition beforeHigh Court, seeking prayer to quash said ECIR, which stand dismissed - Hence, present appeal - Whether impugned proceedings initiated against Petitioners required to be quashed.

Facts:

An FIR came to be registered by CBI against one person, his associates and the officials of three branches of the bank and certain other persons for the offences under Sections 120B, 420, 467, 468, 471, 472 and 474 of Code and Section 13(2) read with 13(1)(d) of Act. It was alleged inter alia in the said FIR that to defraud the bank, the Accused and his associates, in collusion with the officials of bank had misused the KYC documents of his clients/employees/family members as well as the existing customers of the bank to launder the money. The CBI, filed charge-sheet before the Designated CBI Court, against accuse person and some of the officers of the bank for the said offences.Since some of the offences registered by the CBI in the said FIR were scheduled offences under the Prevention of Money Laundering Act, 2002 (PMLA), the Directorate of Enforcement (ED), initiated investigation for the offence of money laundering by registering an Enforcement Case Information Report (ECIR).During the course of investigation, it was revealed that the Petitioner had received more than sum defrauded funds from the accounts of fictitious firms/ companies created and operated by accused person.The Petitioner- Anoop Bartaria therefore filed the writ petition before the High Court, seeking prayer to quash the said ECIR which stand dismissed.

Held, while dismissing the petition:

(i) Section 2(u) defines what is proceeds of crime and Section 2(y) defines what is Scheduled offence. As discernable from the record, the prosecution complaint in ECIR was lodged against the Petitioners and others under the PMLA by the ED, pursuant to the investigation carried out by the CBI and the charge-sheet filed by the CBI against for the offences under Sections 120B, 420, 467, 468, 471, 472 and 474 of Indian Penal Code and Section 13(2) read with Section 13(1)(d) of the Prevention of Corruption Act, 1988 at the Designated CBI Court. All the said offences were scheduled offences within the meaning of Section 2(y) of the said Act. The allegations against the Petitioner No. 1 as the Chairman and Managing Director of company and the Petitioner No. 2 were stated in the prosecution complaint. The Court at this juncture was not required to go into the merits of the said allegations. Suffice it to say that serious allegations of money laundering were alleged against both the Petitioners in the prosecution complaint and sufficient material particulars had been narrated in the said complaint to substantiate the said allegations, which prima facie show the direct involvement of the Petitioners in the alleged offences of money laundering as defined in Section 3 of the said PMLA. [26]

(ii) The Petitioners had also failed to make out any case of abuse of process of the court at the instance of the Respondent authorities. There being enough material to show prima facie involvement of the Petitioners in the alleged offence of money laundering, as contemplated under the PMLA the High Court had rightly dismissed the petitions filed by the Petitioners. As stated in the statement of objects and reasons of the Act, money laundering poses a serious threat not only to the financial systems of the countries but also to their integrity and sovereignty. Hence any lenient view in dealing with such offences would be a travesty of justice. [29]

Disposition: In Favour of State.

• • •

CHAPTER XVI

The Directorate of Enforcement vs. M. Gopal Reddy and Ors. (24.02.2023 – SC) : MANU/SC/0166/2023

Relative Section:

Code of Criminal Procedure, 1973 (CrPC) - Section 438; Indian Penal Code, 1860 (IPC) - Section 120B, Indian Penal Code, 1860 (IPC) - Section 420, Indian Penal Code, 1860 (IPC) - Section 471; Prevention Of Corruption Act, 1988 - Section 7, Prevention Of Corruption Act, 1988 - Section 13(2); Prevention Of Money-laundering Act, 2002 - Section 3, Prevention Of Money-laundering Act, 2002 - Section 4, Prevention Of Money-laundering Act, 2002 - Section 17(1), Prevention Of Money-laundering Act, 2002 - Section 45, Prevention Of Money-laundering Act, 2002 - Section 45(1), Prevention Of Money-laundering Act, 2002 - Section 50

Hon'ble Judges/Coram: M.R. Shah and C.T. Ravikumar, JJ.

Equivalent Citation:2023(2)Crimes2(SC), 2023/INSC/163, 2023(2)J.L.J.R.25,2023(2)MLJ(Crl)135, 2023 (2)PLJR123, [2023]177SCL170(SC)

Number of Pages in the Original Judgment: 8

Case Reference:

Nikesh Tarachand Shah v. Union of India (UOI) and Ors. MANU/SC/1480/2017; P. Chidambaram v. Directorate of Enforcement MANU/SC/1209/2019; Y.S. Jagan Mohan Reddy v. Central Bureau of Investigation MANU/SC/0487/2013; The Asst. Director Enforcement Directorate v. Dr. V.C. Mohan MANU/SC/0193/2022

Case Note:

Criminal - Anticipatory bail - Cancellation of - Sections 3 and 45 of Prevention of Money Laundering Act, 2002 and Section 438 of Code of Criminal Procedure, 1973 - FIR was registered for offence of money laundering under Section 3 of Act, 2002 - Apprehending his arrest in connection with ED case for scheduled offence under Act, 2002, Respondent No. 1 approached High Court by way of anticipatory bail application under Section 438 of Code - High Court had allowed anticipatory bail application and had directed that in case of his arrest in connection with ED case he be released on bail - Hence, present appeal - Whether High Court erred in granting anticipatory bail to Respondent No. 1.

Facts:

The case was registered for the offence of money laundering under Section 3 of the Prevention of Money Laundering Act, 2002.That apprehending his arrest in connection with ED case for the scheduled offence under the Act, 2002, Respondent No. 1 approached the High Court by way of anticipatory bail application under Section 438 Code of Criminal Procedure. The High Court had allowed the anticipatory bail application and had directed that in case of his arrest in connection with ED case he be released on bail.

Held, while allowing the appeal:

(i) By the impugned judgment and order, while granting anticipatory bail the High Court had observed that the provisions of Section 45 of the Act, 2002 shall not be applicable with respect to the anticipatory bail applications/proceedings under Section 438 Code of Criminal Procedure. For which the High Court has relied upon the decision of this Court in the case of Nikesh Tarachand Shah. In the case of Dr. V.C. Mohan, this Court has specifically observed and held that it is the wrong understanding that in the case of Nikesh Tarachand Shah this Court has held that the rigour of Section 45 of the Act, 2002 shall not be applicable to the application under Section 438 Code of Criminal Procedure. In the case of Dr. V.C. Mohan in which the decision of this Court in the case of Nikesh Tarachand Shah was pressed into service, it is specifically observed by this Court that it is one thing to say that Section 45 of the Act, 2002 to offences under the ordinary law would not get attracted but once the prayer for anticipatory bail is made in connection with offence under the Act, 2002, the underlying principles and rigours of Section 45 of the Act, must get triggered-although the application is under Section 438 Code of Criminal Procedure. Therefore, the observations made by the High Court that the provisions of Section 45 of the Act, 2002 shall not be applicable in connection with an application under Section 438 Code of Criminal Procedure was just contrary to the decision in the case of Dr. V.C. Mohan and the same was on misunderstanding of the observations made in the case of Nikesh Tarachand Shah. Once the rigour under Section 45 of the Act, 2002 shall be applicable the impugned judgment and order passed by the High Court granting anticipatory bail to Respondent No. 1 was unsustainable. [5.1]

(ii) Even otherwise on merits also, the impugned judgment and order passed by the High Court granting anticipatory bail to Respondent No. 1 was erroneous and unsustainable. While granting the anticipatory bail to Respondent No. 1 the High Court had not at all considered the nature of allegations and seriousness of the offences alleged of money laundering and the offence(s) under the Act, 2002. Looking to the nature of allegations, it could be said that the same can be said to be very serious allegations of money laundering which were required to be investigated thoroughly. As per the investigating agency, they had collected some material connecting Respondent No. 1 having taken undue advantage from one person. From the impugned judgment and order passed by the High Court, it appears that the High Court had considered the matter, as if, it was dealing with the prayer for anticipatory bail in connection with the ordinary offence under Indian Penal Code. [6]

Disposition: In Favour of State.

• • •

CHAPTER XVII

State Bank of India and Ors. vs. Vijay Mallya (11.07.2022 – SC) : MANU/SC/0842/2022

Relative Section:

Constitution of India - Article 129; Contempt of Courts Act - Section 2; Indian Penal Code, 1860 (IPC) - Section 120B, Indian Penal Code, 1860 (IPC) - Section 420; Prevention Of Corruption Act, 1988 - Section 13(1), Prevention Of Corruption Act, 1988 - Section 13(2); Rules To Regulate Proceedings For Contempt To The Supreme Court, 1975 - Rule 6(1), Supreme Court Rules, 2013

Hon'ble Judges/Coram: U.U.Lalit, S.Ravindra Bhat and Pamidighantam Sri Narasimha, JJ.

Equivalent Citation: III(2022)BC435(SC), 2022 (3) CCC 145 , 2023 (1) Him. LR. 319, 2022 /INSC /700

Number of Pages in the Original Judgment: 14

Case Reference:

Delhi Judicial Service Association, Tis Hazari Court, Delhi v. State of Gujarat and Ors. MANU/SC/0478/1991; State Bank of India and Ors. v. Kingfisher Airlines Ltd. and Ors. MANU/SC/0589/2017; Supreme Court Bar Association v. Union of India (UOI) and Ors. MANU/SC/0291/1998; Noorali Babul Thanewala v. K.M.M. Shetty and Ors. MANU/SC/0077/1990; Rama Narang v. Ramesh Narang and Ors. MANU/SC/1484/2007; Pravin C. Shah v. K.A. Mohd. Ali and Ors. MANU/SC/0622/2001; Chandra Shashi v. Anil Kumar Verma MANU/SC/0558/1995; Dr. Madan Gopal Gupta v. The Agra University and Ors. MANU/UP/0004/1974; Rose v. Laskington MANU/UKWQ/0063/1989 : (1989) 3 AllER 306; Mir v. Mir (1992) 1 AllER 765; Richardson v. Richardson MANU/UKFM/0003/1989 : (1989) 3 AllER 779

Case Note:

Contempt of Courts - Proceedings for recovery of amount - Issue in present case is with regard to transfer of funds in violation of order of court - Whether action on part of the Contemnor in disbursing the amount of US$ 40 million was against the text and tenor of orders passed by the High Court and Contemnor was guilty of contempt?

Facts:

Present Court found Respondent No. 3 (Dr. Vijay Mallya) guilty of committing contempt of Court. The sum of the money which was received by Edmond de Rothschild (Suisse) M.A. was, on the instruction of the Respondent No. 3/contemnor, paid to three trusts wherein the sole beneficiaries were the son and two daughters of the Respondent No. 3/ Contemnor. The aforementioned amount had been transferred in violation of order of court by taking advantage of the very act of contempt which has been held against the Contemnor/Respondent No. 3. It is, therefore, submitted that this Hon'ble Court may give appropriate direction for reversal of the aforesaid transactions by declaring the said transactions to be void. The present contempt proceedings arise out of recovery proceedings by Banks. It is stated by the Counsel on behalf of State Bank of India that decrees have been passed against the Respondent No. 3 in the said recovery proceedings and Recovery Officer has been appointed for enforcement and execution of the said decree. It thought fit, this Hon'ble Court may give appropriate direction to the said Recovery Officer to trace the said funds into the hands of whoever they may have been transferred to and use the same in execution of the decree. In the event the said funds are found inadequate to purge the said contempt, appropriate orders may be passed for sequestration of the assets of the Respondent No. 3/contemnor both in India and outside. Assistance of the Banks and/or the Union of India may be taken to find out all assets that may be available to the Respondent No. 3/Contemnor. Alternatively, a forensic auditor may be appointed to undertake such an exercise.

Held, while disposing of the petition

1. It is well settled that apart from punishing the contemnor for his contumacious conduct, the majesty of law may demand that appropriate directions be issued by the court so that any advantage secured as a result of such contumacious conduct is completely nullified. The approach may require the court to pass directions either for reversal of the transactions in question by declaring said transactions to be void or passing appropriate directions to the concerned authorities to see that the contumacious conduct on the part of the contemnor does not continue to enure to the advantage of the contemnor or any one claiming under him. [13]

2. In its judgment and Order dated 09.05.2017, this Court had found that the action on part of the Contemnor in disbursing the amount of US$ 40 million was against the text and tenor of orders passed by the High Court of

Karnataka and that the Contemnor was guilty of contempt. [14]

3. In the circumstances, in order to maintain the majesty of law, present Court must impose adequate punishment upon the Contemnor and must also pass necessary directions so that the advantages secured by the Contemnor or anyone claiming under him are set at naught and the amounts in question are available in execution of the decrees passed in the concerned Recovery Proceedings. [15]

4. Considering the facts and circumstances on record and the facts that the Contemnor never showed any remorse nor tendered any apology for his conduct, present Court impose sentence of four months and fine in the sum of Rs. 2,000 upon the Contemnor. The fine shall be deposited in the Registry of this Court within four weeks and upon such deposit, the amount shall be made over to the Supreme Court Legal Services Committee. In case the amount of fine is not deposited within the time stipulated, the Contemnor shall undergo further sentence of two months. The Ministry of Home Affairs, Government of India, New Delhi is directed to secure the presence of the Contemnor to undergo the imprisonment imposed upon him. Government of India including the Ministry of External Affairs and all other agencies or instrumentalities shall carry out the directions issued by this Court with due diligence and utmost expediency. [16]

5. The transactions referred to in the judgment and Order dated 09.05.2017 in terms of which the amount of US$ 40 million was disbursed to the beneficiaries detailed in paragraph 16 of the said judgment and order is held to be void and inoperative. The Contemnor and the beneficiaries under said transactions referred to in the said Paragraph 16 shall be bound to deposit the amount received by such beneficiaries along with interest at the rate of 8 per cent per annum with the concerned Recovery Officer within four weeks. In case the amounts are not so deposited, the concerned Recovery Officer shall be entitled to take appropriate proceedings for recovery of said amounts; and Government of India and all the concerned agencies shall extend assistance and complete cooperation. It shall be open to take such appropriate steps including the appointment of Forensic Auditor(s). [17]

6. Contempt petitions disposed off. [19]

Disposition: Disposed of

Industry: Banks

• • •

CHAPTER XVIII

Kanchan Kumar vs. The State of Bihar (14.09.2022 – SC) : MANU/SC/1164/2022

Relative Section:

Code of Criminal Procedure, 1973 (CrPC) - Section 227, Code of Criminal Procedure, 1973 (CrPC) - Section 228, Code of Criminal Procedure, 1973 (CrPC) - Section 239, Prevention Of Corruption Act, 1988 - Section 13(1), Prevention Of Corruption Act, 1988 - Section 13(2)

Hon'ble Judges/Coram: B.R. Gavai and Pamidighantam Sri Narasimha, JJ.

Equivalent Citation: 2023(1)ACR211,2022(238)AIC248,AIR2022SC4288, 2022 (121) ACC 653,2022(5) BLJ373, 2022(3)Crimes448(SC), 2022(4)CriminalCC200, 2022(5)CTC466, 2022/INSC/955, 2023 (1) MWN (CR.) 1, 2022(4)RCR(Criminal)737, (2022)9SCC577

Number of Pages in the Original Judgment: 8

Case Reference:

Union of India (UOI) v. Prafulla Kumar Samal and Ors. MANU/SC/0414/1978; Sajjan Kumar v. Central Bureau of Investigation MANU/SC/0741/2010; Dipakbhai Jagdishchandra Patel v. State of Gujarat and Ors. MANU/SC/0595/2019; Ghulam Hassan Beigh v. Mohammad Maqbool Magrey MANU/SC/0920/2022

Case Note:

Criminal - Entitlement to discharge - Present appeal is against the concurrent dismissals by the trial and the High Court of the application for discharge filed by the Appellant under Section 227 of the Code of Criminal Procedure, 1973 - Whether the Appellant is entitled to be discharged of the proceedings initiated against him under the Prevention of Corruption Act, 1988 (PC Act)?

Facts:

The Appellant applied for discharge before the Court of Special Judge alleging that there were glaring errors in the calculation. However, the Court summarily dismissed the application by its order. Aggrieved by the dismissal of his application for discharge, the Appellant moved the High

Court. After recounting the chronology of events, the High Court proceeded to quote judgment after judgment, and finally dismissed the revision application. It is submitted that, the basic objection relating to the calculation and wrongful inclusion of certain items was sufficient for the Trial Court to discharge the Appellant.

Held, while allowing the appeal

1. The Special Judge (Vigilance) dismissed the discharge application on the simple ground that a roving inquiry is not permitted at the stage of discharge. What present Court have undertaken is not a roving inquiry, but a simple and necessary inquiry for a proper adjudication of an application for discharge. The Special Judge (Vigilance) was bound to conduct a similar inquiry for coming to a conclusion that a prima facie case is made out for the Appellant to stand trial. Unfortunately, the High Court committed the same mistake as that of the Special Judge (Vigilance). [18]

2. The allegation relating to Appellant's disproportionate income in the period between 1974 and 1988 was levelled in an FIR filed twelve years after the said period concluded. The charge-sheet came to be filed seven years after the registration of the FIR. The application for discharge came to be dismissed on 28.03.2016, almost after a decade of filing of the charge sheet. The dismissal was affirmed by the High Court seven months thereafter, i.e., on 05.10.2016. Finally, and most unfortunately, the present SLP has been pending before this Court for the last six years. In the meanwhile, the Appellant superannuated from service in 2010, but had no option except to contest the case. He is now 72 years. Continuation of the prosecution, apart from the illegality would also be unjust. [19]

3. Order of the High Court and that of the Court of Special Judge is set aside and the Appellant is discharged. Appeal allowed. [20]

Disposition: In Favour of Accused.

• • •

CHAPTER XIX

The State of Jammu and Kashmir and Ors. vs. Saleem Ur Rehman (29.10.2021 – SC) : MANU/SC/1022/2021

Relative Section:

Code of Criminal Procedure, 1898 (CrPC) - Section 190, Code of Criminal Procedure, 1898 (CrPC) - Section 190(1), Code of Criminal Procedure, 1898 (CrPC) - Section 193, Code of Criminal Procedure, 1898 (CrPC) - Section 195, Code of Criminal Procedure, 1898 (CrPC) - Section 196, Code of Criminal Procedure, 1898 (CrPC) - Section 197, Code of Criminal Procedure, 1898 (CrPC) - Section 198, Code of Criminal Procedure, 1898 (CrPC) - Section 199, Code of Criminal Procedure, 1898 (CrPC) - Section 537; Code of Criminal Procedure, 1973 (CrPC) - Section 3, Code of Criminal Procedure, 1973 (CrPC) - Section 4, Code of Criminal Procedure, 1973 (CrPC) - Section 5, Code of Criminal Procedure, 1973 (CrPC) - Section 56, Code of Criminal Procedure, 1973 (CrPC) - Section 154, Code of Criminal Procedure, 1973 (CrPC) - Section 155, Code of Criminal Procedure, 1973 (CrPC) - Section 155(1), Code of Criminal Procedure, 1973 (CrPC) - Section 155(4), Code of Criminal Procedure, 1973 (CrPC) - Section 156(1), Code of Criminal Procedure, 1973 (CrPC) - Section 156(2), Code of Criminal Procedure, 1973 (CrPC) - Section 156(3), Code of Criminal Procedure, 1973 (CrPC) - Section 173; Code of Criminal Procedure (CrPC), Samvat 1989 - Section 56, Code of Criminal Procedure (CrPC), Samvat 1989 - Section 155; Constitution of India - Article 226, Constitution of India - Article 227; Indian Penal Code, 1860 (IPC) - Section 161, Indian Penal Code, 1860 (IPC) - Section 165, Indian Penal Code, 1860 (IPC) - Section 165A; Jammu and Kashmir Prevention of Corruption Act, 1949 - Section 3, Jammu and Kashmir Prevention of Corruption Act, 1949 - Section 5(1), Jammu and Kashmir Prevention of Corruption Act, 1949 - Section 5(2); Jammu and Kashmir Vigilance Manual, 2008 - Rule 3.16; Prevention Of Corruption Act, 1947 - Section 3, Prevention Of Corruption Act, 1947 - Section 5, Prevention Of Corruption Act, 1947 - Section 5A, Prevention Of Corruption Act, 1947 - Section 5(1), Prevention Of Corruption Act, 1947 - Section 5A(1), Prevention Of Corruption Act, 1947

- Section 5(2), Prevention Of Corruption Act, 1947 - Section 5(4); Prevention Of Corruption Act, 1988 - Section 13, Prevention Of Corruption Act, 1988 - Section 13(1), Prevention Of Corruption Act, 1988 - Section 17, Prevention Of Corruption Act, 1988 - Section 23(2), Prevention of Corruption Act, 1988 - Section 5A; Ranbir Penal Code, 1989 - Section 120B

Hon'ble Judges/Coram: M.R. Shah and A.S. Bopanna, JJ.

Equivalent Citation: 2021 (3) ALT (Crl.) 460 (A.P.), 2021(4)Crimes233(SC), 2021/INSC/703, 2022 (1)J.L.J.R.128, 2021(6)JKJ50[SC], 2021(3)N.C.C.727, 2022(1)PLJR8, 2021(4) RCR (Criminal) 671, [2021]10SCR864

Number of Pages in the Original Judgment: 20

Case Reference:

Lalita Kumari v. Govt. of U.P. and Ors. MANU/SC/1166/2013; State of Haryana and Ors. v. Ch. Bhajan Lal and Ors. MANU/SC/0115/1992; State of Madhya Pradesh and Ors. v. Ram Singh MANU/SC/0064/2000; S.N. Mukherjee v. Union of India (UOI) MANU/SC/0346/1990; Union of India (UOI) and Ors. v. E.G. Nambudiri MANU/SC/0293/1991; ORYX Fisheries Private Limited v. Union of India (UOI) and Ors. MANU/SC/0921/2010; Special Land Acquisition Officer, Bombay and Ors. v. Godrej and Boyce MANU/SC/0560/1987; Indian National Congress (I) v. Institute of Social Welfare and Ors. MANU/SC/0451/2002; Pravin Chandra Mody v. State of Andhra Pradesh MANU/SC/0082/1964; State of Punjab v. Brij Lal Palta MANU/SC/0389/1968; Satya Narain Musadi and Ors. v. State of Bihar MANU/SC/0234/1979; Madan Lal v. State of Punjab MANU/SC/0369/1967; Bhanwar Singh and Ors. v. State of Rajasthan MANU/SC/0057/1967; Nazir Ahmad v. Emperor MANU/PR/0111/1936; State of Uttar Pradesh v. Singhara Singh and Ors. MANU/SC/0082/1963; Priyanka Srivastava and Ors. v. State of U.P. and Ors. MANU/SC/0344/2015; H.N. Rishbud and Ors. v. State of Delhi MANU/SC/0049/1954; Parbhu v. Emperor MANU/PR/0035/1944; Taylor v. Taylor, (1875) 1 Ch.D, 426; Lumbhardar Zutshi v. R. AIR 1950 PC 26; Ram Krishna Dalmia v. State AIR (1958) Pb. 172

Case Note:

Criminal - Quashing of proceedings -FIR registered under Section 5(1)(d) read with 5(2) of the J&K Prevention of Corruption Act, 2006 (J&K PC Act) - Section 120B of the Ranbir Penal Code (RPC) -Respondent alleged of misappropriation of government money by effecting purchases of sub-standard medical kits at highly exorbitant rates - High Court by impugned judgment quashed criminal proceedings and declared Rule 3.16

of the Vigilance Manual, 2008 in direct conflict with the Constitution Bench Judgment in the case of LalitaKumari v. Government of Uttar Pradesh - Subject provision declared ultra vires - Hence, the present appeal by State - Whether High Court by impugned judgment erred in quashing proceedings and declaring Rule 3.16 of the Vigilance Manual, 2008ultravires?

Facts:

In the instead case, FIR was registered against the Respondent alleging that during 2010-11, the Director Health Services, Kashmir along with the other Accused persons misappropriated the huge amount of government money by way of effecting purchases of sub-standard medical kits under National Rural Health Mission (NRHM) at highly exorbitant rates and in violation of the conditions of supply orders placed by the department. High Court vide impugned judgment quashed entire proceedings and hence the present appeal.

Held, while allowing the Appeal:

Offence under the Prevention of Corruption Act is a substantive offence and the investigation in respect of the offence under the PC Act, when considered and coupled with the offence of conspiracy, there is no requirement of prior sanction of the Magistrate. Merely because the offence of the conspiracy may be involved, investigation into the substantive offence, i.e., in the present case, offence under the PC Act which is cognizable is not required to await a sanction from the Magistrate, as that would lead to a considerable delay and affect the investigation and it will derail the investigation. Therefore, the High Court has erred in quashing the criminal proceedings on the ground that as the offence under Section 120B which is a non-cognizable, prior sanction as required under Section 155 of J&K Code of Criminal Procedure is not obtained.[10]

As per Clause 3.16 only after the Preliminary Enquiry is conducted and there is a prima facie case found, an FIR is required to be registered. Considering the nature of offences, a detailed enquiry is required and therefore it is observed in Clause 3.16 that a PE should be completed normally within a period of six months. It is the case on behalf of the Respondent and even as observed and held by the High Court in the impugned judgment and order as per the law laid down by this Court in the case of LalitaKumari, a detailed investigation into the allegations on merits is not required by holding Preliminary Enquiry and that such enquiry is to be completed within a period of 7 days is concerned, it is to be noted that in the case of LalitaKumari, it is not held that if the Preliminary Enquiry is not completed within a period of 7 days, the entire criminal proceedings would be void and the same are to be quashed.[12]

While holding a Preliminary Enquiry under Clause 3.16, whatever is conducted will be in the form of enquiry into the allegations to consider whether any prima facie case is made out or not which requires further investigation after registering the FIR or not. While considering the prima facie case for the purpose of registering the FIR, some enquiry/investigation is bound to be there, however, the same shall be only for the purpose of finding out a prima facie case for the purpose of registration of the FIR only. Merely because while holding a Preliminary Enquiry a detailed enquiry is made into the allegations made against the Respondent which, as observed hereinabove, can be said to be only for the purpose of finding out a prima facie case for the purpose of registration of the FIR and merely because some more time is taken in conducting the Preliminary Enquiry before registering the FIR, the entire criminal proceedings cannot be quashed. High Court has materially erred in holding and declaring Clause 3.16 as ultra vires.[13]

Impugned judgment and order passed by the High Court quashing the entire criminal proceedings and quashing and setting aside the Entrustment Order authorising the Inspector to investigate the FIR and holding and declaring Rule/Clause 3.16 of the Vigilance Manual, 2008 dealing with Preliminary Enquiry (PE) as ultra vires is unsustainable and thus quashed and set aside.[15]

Appeal allowed.[16]

Disposition: In Favour of State

• • •

The State by S.P. through the Spe. CBI vs. Uttamchand Bohra (09.12.2021 – SC) : MANU/SC/1214/2021

Relative Section:

Code of Criminal Procedure, 1973 (CrPC) - Section 161, Code of Criminal Procedure, 1973 (CrPC) - Section 173, Code of Criminal Procedure, 1973 (CrPC) - Section 209, Code of Criminal Procedure, 1973 (CrPC) - Section 226, Code of Criminal Procedure, 1973 (CrPC) - Section 227, Code of Criminal Procedure, 1973 (CrPC) - Section 228, Code of Criminal Procedure, 1973 (CrPC) - Section 239, Code of Criminal Procedure, 1973 (CrPC) - Section 397, Code of Criminal Procedure, 1973 (CrPC) - Section 401; Indian Penal Code, 1860 (IPC) - Section 107, Indian Penal Code, 1860 (IPC) - Section 109, Indian Penal Code, 1860 (IPC) - Section 120A, Indian Penal Code, 1860 (IPC) - Section 120B; Prevention Of Corruption Act, 1988 - Section 7, Prevention Of Corruption Act, 1988 - Section 13(1), Prevention Of Corruption Act, 1988 - Section 13(2)

Hon'ble Judges/Coram: K.M. Joseph and S. Ravindra Bhat, JJ.

Equivalent Citation:2022 (2) ALT (Crl.) 188 (A.P.), 2022(2)BLJ195, 2021(4)Crimes521(SC), 2022 (1)CriminalCC184, 2021/INSC/855, 2022(1)JKJ323[SC], 2022(1)N.C.C.42, 2022(1)RCR(Criminal)317, [2021]9SCR821

Number of Pages in the Original Judgment: 14

Case Reference:

Nirmaljit Singh Hoon v. The State of West Bengal and Ors. MANU/SC/0196/1972; State of Bihar v. Ramesh Singh MANU/SC/0139/1977; Union of India (UOI) v. Prafulla Kumar Samal and Ors. MANU/SC/0414/1978; Central Bureau of Investigation, Hyderabad v. K. Narayana Rao MANU/SC/0774/2012; P. Vijayan v. State of Kerala and Ors. MANU/SC/0058/2010; Sajjan Kumar v. Central Bureau of Investigation MANU /SC /0741 /2010; State of Jammu and Kashmir v. Sudershan Chakkar and Ors. MANU/SC/0383/1995; P. Nallammal and Ors. v. State Rep. by Inspector of Police MANU/SC/0455/1999; Alka Bose v. Parmatma Devi and Ors. MANU /SC /8475/2008; Deepak Surana v. State of M.P.

Case Note:

Criminal - Quashing - Complaint alleging abatement of conspiracy with public servant -Sections 109, 120B of the Indian Penal Code, 1860 (IPC) and Section 13(2) read with Section 13(1)(e) of the Prevention of Corruption Act, 1988 (PCA) - Accused alleged of amassing wealth disproportionate to income -High Court quashed chargesheet filed holding mere in possession of document could not incriminate him - Hence, the present appeal - Whether High Court erred in quashing the charge sheet in question?

Facts:

High Court vide impugned judgment quashed charge sheet against the Respondent (Accused No. 5 before the Trial Court). Trial court had earlier rejected application under Section 239 of the Code of Criminal Procedure seeking his discharge.Accused was alleged of abetting and/or conspiring with the principal Accused, a public servant (A-1), so as to permit him to accumulate assets disproportionate to his known sources of income. Hence, the present appeal by State.

Held, while dismissing the Appeal:

The factual narration in this case would reveal that the Respondent, was not a public officer or public servant. He cannot therefore, be charged with committing an offence Under Section 13(1)(e) read with Section 13(2) of the PCA. There is no allegation that he received any monetary or other benefit, or that he held the property in his name for the benefit of A-1. [23]

The chargesheet further does not contain any allegation which can amount to an offence under Section 109 Indian Penal Code. The prosecution has not suggested that he abetted A-1 to acquire disproportionate assets in any manner; the only allegation is that the title deeds to the flat, which is in the name of M/s. Raviteja Trading Co. Pvt. Ltd. was seized from his custody and that he had instructed his employee to witness the document. An allegation of the existence of signatures of as a witness to the sale deed cannot amount to his aiding or abetting A-1 to acquire disproportionate assets. Witnessing a sale deed is a formal requirement. Likewise, the fact that the sale deed was in his residence cannot satisfy the ingredient of any of the offences alleged against him.[24]

The FIR in the present case names only A-1 and A-2 as the Accused. The sale deed had already been seized from Respondent's house by then.[27]

The present appeal lacks merit. It is therefore dismissed.[33]

Disposition: In Favour of Accused.

• • •

74

Maars Software International Ltd. and Ors. vs. Union of India (UOI) and Ors. (22.04.2019 – SC) : MANU/SC/0579/2019

Relative Section:

Foreign Exchange Management Act, 1999 - Section 8,Section 13,Section 16(3),Section 35, Section 42,

Section 42(1); Foreign Exchange Management (Realization, Repatriation and Surrender of Foreign Exchange)

Regulations, 2000 - Regulation 3, Foreign Exchange Management (Realization, Repatriation and Surrender of

Foreign Exchange) Regulations, 2000 - Regulation 9

Hon'ble Judges/Coram: Abhay Manohar Sapre and Dinesh Maheshwari, JJ.

Equivalent Citation:AIR2019SC2849, [2019]214CompCas485(SC), (2020)1CompLJ473(SC), 2019 (366)

ELT598(S.C.), 2019/INSC/550, 2019(6)SCALE570, (2019)11SCC291, [2019]153SCL385(SC)

Number of Pages in the Original Judgment: 4

Case Reference: nil

Case Note:

FEMA - Violation of provision - Validity of complaint - Enforcement Directorate filed complaint, against

Appellant-Company before Special Director of Enforcement - Complaint was found on material collected

during course of investigation made in affairs and dealings of Appellant-Company in their business operations -

Special Director allowed complaint and held that Appellant-Company had contravened provisions of FEMA

and imposed penalty - On appeal, Tribunal set aside order of Special Director - On further appeal, High Court

set aside order of Tribunal and restored order of Adjudicating Authority - Hence, present appeal - Whether High

Court erred in setting aside order of Tribunal relating to validity of complaint.

Facts:

The Enforcement Directorate filed a complaint, under Section 16 (3) of the Foreign Exchange Management Act,

1999 against the Appellant-Company before the Special Director of Enforcement (Adjudicating Authority). The

complaint was founded on the material collected during the course of detailed investigation made in the affairs

and the dealings of the Appellant-Company in their business operations. The Special Director allowed the

complaint and held that the Appellant-Company had contravened the provisions of FEMA and accordingly

imposed a penalty. On appeal, the Tribunal set aside the order and directed the authorities to refund the amount

which was deposited by the Appellants in these proceedings for filing the appeals. On further appeal, the High

Court allowed the appcals, set aside the order of the Tribunal and restored the order of the Adjudicating

Authority.

Held, while allowing the appeal:

(i) The Appellants had filed material, in the case, with a view to show as to what steps they had taken to realize

and repatriate the dues in question. [19]

(ii) It was clear that the High Court did not examine the case of the parties in the context of material placed by

the Appellants. [20]

(iii) The High Court should have taken into consideration the said material with a view to decide as to whether

it was relevant or/and sufficient, and whether it could justify the Appellants' case as contemplated under Section

8 of FEMA. [21]

(iv) Instead, the High Court seemed to have proceeded on wrong assumption that since the Appellants did not

file any material, a case was made out against them. This observation of the High Court, was contrary to the

record of the case and hence, interference in the impugned order was called for. [22]

(v) Thus, remand the case to the High Court and request the High Court to decide the appeal afresh on merits in
accordance with law. [23]
Disposition: Appeal Allowed

• • •

Adv. Jayprakash Somani's Videos On Law

Adv. Jayprakash Somani's Videos on Law on Youtube- 'jaysomani64' channel.

1) SLP in Supreme Court / Special Leave Petitions in the Supreme Court of India

2) Transfer of Civil & Criminal Cases by the Supreme Court of India / Transfer of Matrimonial Cases

3) Appellate Jurisdiction of the Supreme Court of India

4) Jurisdictions of the Supreme Court of India

5) Public Interest Litigation in the Supreme Court of India / PIL in Supreme Court

6) Article 32 Writ Petitions in the Supreme Court of India

7) Bail Matters Top 10 Supreme Court Cases

8) FIR Quashing in High Court & Supreme Court

9) Bail & Anticipatory Bail Matters in Supreme Court

10) Insolvency & Bankruptcy Matters in the Supreme Court

11) Insolvency & Bankruptcy Code 2016 Part 1

12) Insolvency & Bankruptcy Code 2016 Part 2

13) Insolvency & Bankruptcy Code 2016 Part 3

14) Corporate Liquidation Process

15) Supreme Court Rules & Procedures Webinar of 2.5 hour on Zoom

16) RDDBFI Act, 1993 (Introduction)

17) The Indian Contact Act 1872

18) Negotiable Instruments Act (Introduction)

19) How to avoid matrimonial disputes& some more videos

20) SEBI Matters in the Supreme Court

21) Matrimonial Matters: Supreme Court's 20 Case Laws

22) Consumer Matters Supreme Court's 20 Case Laws

23) Service Matters Supreme Court's 20 Case Laws

24) How to Search Lawyer for Your Matter

25) Property Matters Supreme Court's 20 Case Laws

26) Bail Matters: Supreme Court's 20 Case Laws

27) Supreme Court / High Court Vacation Benches

28) 69000 Teacher's Recruitment Matters of UP Government in the Supreme Court

29) Contempt of Court Matters in the Supreme Court

30) Advocate Act's Matters in the Supreme Court

31) Business Law Matters in the Supreme Court

32) Banking Matters in the Supreme Court

33) Labour Law Matters in the Supreme Court

34) Arbitration Matters in the Supreme Court

35) Careers in Law -Zoom Webinar by Adv. Jayprakash Somani

36) Civil Matters in the Supreme Court

37) Consumer Protection Act | Consumer Matters in the Supreme Court

38) Corporate Matters in the Supreme Court

39) Criminal Matters in the Supreme Court

40) Role of Respondent in the Supreme Court of India

41) Motor Vehicle Accident Matters in Supreme Court with case laws

42) Article 131 Original Suits in Supreme Court

43) PIL in Supreme Court/ Public Interest Litigations in the Supreme Court of India'

44) CAB Citizenship Amendment Bill is not Unconstitutional

45) Supreme Court of India Cases & Process – Marathi

46) Legal Services Export / Export of Legal Services

47) Transfer of Matrimonial Cases by the Supreme Court of India

48) Public Interest Litigation PIL

49) The Specific Relief Act (Introduction)

50) Corporate Insolvency Resolution Process CIRP

51) ABMM's Career 5 - Careers in Law

52) Transfer of cases by Supreme Court

53) Writ Petitions in High Court & Supreme Court of India

54) Supreme Court Jurisdictions - Appeals, SLP, Writ Petitions, Transfer, Original, Review, Curative

55) LEGAL INDIA TV Show: Cases Handled in Supreme Court

56) Corporate Liquidation Process

57) Legal Services Export / Export of Legal Services

58) Corporate Laws

59) Election Matters- Supreme Court's 20 Case Laws

60) Companies Act, 2013

62) Competition Act, 2002

63) Banking Matters - Supreme Court's 20 Case Laws

64) Election Matters in the Supreme Court

65) Armed Forces Tribunal Matters in the Supreme Court

66) Compassionate Appointment Service matter

67)Foreign Exchange Management Act FEMA

68)Foreign Trade Policy 2021-26 Proposed

69)Customs Act 1962

70)Narcotic Drugs and Psychotropic Substances Act, 1985 NDPS Act

71)Foreign Trade Development & Regulation Act, 1992

72)How to Search Good Advocate in the Supreme Court of India

73)Sr. Adv Vikas Singh's Interview in Nani Palkhivala Wednesday Law Club

74)Indian Penal Code (I. P. C.)

75)Criminal Procedure Code (Cr. P. C.)

76)Commercial Courts & International Arbitration - by Mr. Jaideep Gupta, Senior Advocate in Nani Palkhivala Wednesday Law Club

77)Sr. Adv Ranji Thomos in Nani Palkhivala Wednesday Law Club

78)Urgent Matters in Supreme Court during vacations

79)498A Bail Matters in Supreme Court

81)376 Bail Matters in Supreme Court

82)302, 304, 307, 308 Bail Matters in Supreme Court

83)138, 420 Bail Matters in Supreme Court

84)POCSO Act Bail Matters in Supreme Court

85)NDPS Act Bail Matters in Supreme Court

86)What is ED (Enforcement Directorate)?

87)Prevention of Money Laundering Act, 2002 (PMLA Act)

88)Insolvency & Bankruptcy Code- Supreme Court Case Laws. Webinar in Nani Palkhivala Wednesday Law Club

89)What is NCLT & NCLAT?

90)Acquittal from 376- Supreme Court's some case laws in Nani Palkhivala Wednesday Law Club dt 28.7.22

91)Insolvency & Bankruptcy in India

92)Can we file case directly in the Supreme Court?

93)Adv. Anuja Pethia has cleared AOR Exam 2021 with 77% marks - Her interview in Nani Palkhivala Wednesday Law Club

94)Customs Act - Supreme Court Case Laws & Interview of AOR Adv. Anuja Pethia in Nani Palkhivala Law Club.

95)The Uttar Pradesh Public Service Tribunals Act, 1976

96)POCSO Act - Supreme Court Case Laws & Interview of AOR Adv. Shoumendu Mukharji & Adv. Nishant Verma in Nani Palkhivala Law Club.

97)Who Can Trigger CIRP Process Under Insolvency Law of India

98) The Uttar Pradesh Government Servant Discipline and Appeal Rules, 1999

99) CIRP Application Under Sec 7 by FC

100) Information Technology Act 2000

101) Uttar Pradesh Recruitment of Dependants of Government Servants Dying in Harness Rules, 1974

102) Foreign Exchange Management Act 1999 & Supreme Court's Case Laws on FEMA & Leading Case of AOR Exam in Nani Palkhivala Law Club.

103) Arbitration and Conciliation Act 1996 & It's Supreme Court Case Laws in Nani Palkhivala Wednesday Law Club.

104) Narcotic Drugs & Psychotropic Substances Act 1985 (NDPS Act) & It's Supreme Court Case Laws in Nani Palkhivala Wednesday Law Club.

105) Recovery of Debts and Bankruptcy Act 1993

106) Uttar Pradesh Land Revenue Code 2006

107) CIRP Application Under Sec 9 by OC

108) CIRP Application Under Sec 10 by CD

109) Hindu Succession Act, 1956

110) Maharashtra Civil Services Rules, 1981

111) Indian Contract Act, 1872 & Supreme Court's Case Laws" in Nani Palkhiwala Wednesday Law Club

112) Securities and Exchange Board of India Act, 1992 i. e. SEBI Act 1992 & Case Laws on Insiders Trading" in Nani Palkhiwala Wednesday Law Club

113) Moratorium Under Section 14 of IBC, 2016

114) Hindu Marriage Act, 1955

115) Maharashtra Land Revenue Code, 1966

116) 64 Leading Cases of AOR Exam Session 1 :- Cases 1 to16 in Nani Palkhiwala Wednesday Law Club

117) 64 Leading Cases of AOR Exam Session 2: Cases 17 to 32 in Nani Palkhivala Wednesday Law Club

118) 64 Leading Cases of AOR Examination Session 3: Cases 33 to 48 in Nani Palkhivala Wednesday Law Club

119) 64 Leading Cases of AOR Exam Session 4: Cases 49 to 64 in Nani Palkhivala Wednesday Law Club

120) Labour Laws of India: Part 1 - 4 New Labour Law Codes of India

121) New Labour Laws Part 2 The Code on Wages, 2019

122) New Labour Laws Part 3:- The Code on Social Security, 2020

123) Argue in English Fluently & Confidently - Two months online course.

124) SLP Admission in the Supreme Court. 2023 (Hindi)

125) Transfer of Petitions from the Supreme Court (Hindi)

126) Review Petition in the Supreme Court.(Hindi)

127) Recovery of debts from the Company (Hindi)

128) How to search 'Good Insolvency & Bankruptcy Consultant?' (HINDI)

129) Curative Petition in the Supreme Court

130) AFT Appeals in the Supreme Court (HINDI)

131) NCLAT's Appeals in the Supreme Court.

132) Transfer Petition: Which matters can we transfer?

133) SLP Types of SLP in the Supreme court of India (English).

134) Argue in English Fluently and Confidently in the High Court & Supreme Court'.

• • •

List Of Adv. Jayprakash Somani's Published Books

List of Adv. Jayprakash Somani's Published Books

1. Supreme Court of India's Leading Case Laws on 'Insolvency & Bankruptcy Code 2016'
2. Bail Matters – Supreme Court's Latest Leading Case Laws
3. Arbitration Matters- Supreme Court's Latest Leading Case Laws
4. Property Matters - Supreme Court's Latest Leading Case Laws
5. Matrimonial Matters- Supreme Court's Latest Leading Case Laws
6. Election Matters- Supreme Court's Latest Leading Case Laws
7. SEBI Matters- Supreme Court's Latest Leading Case Laws
8. Banking Matters- Supreme Court's Latest Leading Case Laws
9. Service Matters- Supreme Court's Latest Leading Case Laws
10. Contempt of Court Matters- Supreme Court's Latest Leading Case Laws
11. Consumer Protection Matters- Supreme Court's Latest Leading Case Laws
12. Corporate Law- Supreme Court's Latest Leading Case Laws
13. Supreme Court's AOR Exam- Leading Cases
14. Armed Force Tribunal - Supreme Court's Latest Leading Case Laws
15. Acquittal From 376 - Supreme Court's Latest Leading Case Laws
16. Negotiable instrument – Supreme Court's Latest Leading Case Laws
17. Contract Act- Supreme Court's Latest Leading Case Laws
18. Insider trading- Supreme Court's Latest Leading Case Laws
19. Foreign Exchange and Management Act- Supreme Court's Latest Leading Case Laws
20. Income Tax Act- Supreme Court's Latest Leading Case Laws
21. Company Law- Supreme Court's Latest Leading Case Laws
22. Competition & Monopoly Matters- Supreme Court's Latest Leading Case Laws
23. Compassionate Appointment- Service Matters- Supreme Court's Latest Leading Case Laws
24. Compulsory Retirement- Service Matters- Supreme Court's Latest Leading Case Laws
25. Voluntary Retirement- Service Matters- Supreme Court's Latest Leading Case Laws
26. Removal/Dismissal/Termination from Service- Supreme Court's Latest

Leading Case Laws

27. Seniority- Service Matter- Supreme Court's Latest Leading Case Laws
28. Promotion- Service Matter- Supreme Court's Latest Leading Case Laws
29. Equal Pay for Equal Work- Service Matter- Supreme Court's Latest Leading Case Laws
30. Condition of Service- Service Matter- Supreme Court's Latest Leading Case Laws
31. Customs Act- Supreme Court's Leading Case Laws
32. Information Technology Act- Supreme Court's Leading Case Laws
33. SEC. 125 CR. P. C.- Supreme Court's Leading Case Laws
34. SEC. 498A OF I. P. C.- Supreme Court's Leading Case Laws
35. MOTOR VEHICLE ACT- Supreme Court's Leading Case Laws
36. CONDITION OF SERVICE- SERVICE MATTER- Supreme Court's Leading Case Laws
37. SUSPENSION- SERVICE MATTER- Supreme Court's Leading Case Laws
38. Reservation in SC, ST, OBC- Service Matter- Supreme Court's Leading Case Laws
39. NARCOTIC DRUGS AND PSYCHOTROPIC SUBSTANCES (NDPS) ACT - Supreme Court of India's Latest Leading Case Laws
40. SEC 302 IPC - Supreme Court of India's Latest Leading Case Laws
41. PROTECTION OF CHILDREN FROM SEXUAL OFFENCES ACT (POCSO) - Supreme Court of India's Latest Leading Case Laws
42. PMLA ACT BAIL MATTERS - Supreme Court of India's Leading Case Laws
43. SEC 376 BAIL MATTERS - Supreme Court of India's Leading Case Laws
44. SEC 302 BAIL MATTERS - Supreme Court of India's Leading Case Laws
45. POCSO ACT BAIL MATTERS - Supreme Court of India's Leading Case Laws
46. JUVENILE JUSTICE ACT- Supreme Court of India's Leading Case Laws
47. TRANSFER OF PROPERTY ACT- Supreme Court of India's Leading Case Laws
48. PROFESSIONAL ETHICS OF ADVOCATES- AOR EXAM- SUPREME COURT'S LEADING CASE LAWS
49. WHITE COLLAR CRIME- SUPREME COURT'S LEADING CASE LAWS
50. SEC 302 BAIL MATTERS- SUPREME COURT'S LEADING CASE LAWS
51. SEC 7 IBC 2016 - SUPREME COURT'S LATEST LEADING CASE LAW
52. ADVERSE POSSESSION IN PROPERTY MATTER - SUPREME COURT'S LATEST LEADING CASE LAWS

53. FOOD SAFETY AND STANDARD ACT 2006' - SUPREME COURT AND HIGH COURT's LEADING CASE LAWS

54. ARMED FORCE TRIBUNAL ACT- SUPREME COURT'S LATEST LEADING CASE LAWS

55. ESSENTIAL COMMODITIES ACT 1955- SUPREME COURT'S LATEST LEADING CASE LAWS

56. FOREIGN TRADE DEVELOPMENT AND REGULATION ACT'- SUPREME COURT AND HIGH COURT'S LEADING CASE LAWS

57. PARTNERSHIP ACT 1932- SUPREME COURT'S LEADING CASE LAWS

58. COTPA ACT 2003 - SUPREME COURT AND HIGH COURT'S LEADING CASE LAWS

59. DOMESTIC VIOLENCE ACT 2005 - SUPREME COURT'S LEADING CASE LAWS

60. DOWRY PROHIBITION ACT 1961 - SUPREME COURT'S LATEST CASE LAWS

61. SUPREME COURT'S AOR EXAM- DRAFTING Formates of more than 25 Drafts for AOR Exam Paper 2 - Drafting

62. SPECIFIC RELIEF ACT 1963- SUPREME COURT'S LATEST LEADING CASE LAWS

63. PREVENTION OF MONEY LAUNDERING ACT 2002- SUPREME COURT'S LATEST CASE LAWS

Books are available online in India
1. Notion Press: https://notionpress.com/author/jayprakash_somani
2. Amazon: https://www.amazon.in/s?k=jayprakash+somani
3. Flipkart: https://www.flipkart.com/search?q=Jayprakash%20Somani
Books are available online at International Market
4. Amazon International: https://www.amazon.com/s?k=jayprakash+somani
5. Amazon United Kingdom: https://www.amazon.co.uk/s?k=jayprakash+somani
6. E-Books/Kindle edition at National & International Level: https://www.amazon.in/s?k=jaypraksh+somani

• • •

Adv Jayprakash Somani's Online Legal & Import Export Courses

Download our app to get access to our Free Videos, Free Bare Acts, Free Study Material in Legal as well as International Business Regime.

Android App Link ;-https://clpandrea.page.link/cmSm

Ios APp Link :-https://apps.apple.com/us/app/classplus/id1324522260

Login with org code ;- (qywzji)

Web Link ;-https://qywzji.courses.store/

Download App on Google play store - Type

Jayprakash Somani SupremeCourt

Legal Courses :

1. SLP- Bail Matters- Drafting & Successful Arguing in the Supreme Court.

2. SLP- Succession Matters- Drafting & Successful Arguing in the

Supreme Court.

3. Legal Vocabulary & its practice pattern to Argue in High Court and Supreme Court / Improve Your Legal English.

4. SLP- Property Matters - Drafting and Successful Arguing in the Supreme Court.

International Business Courses -

1. Agri Products Exports - Scope from India.

2. Textile Exports - Scope from India.

3. Export Import Procedure -Perfect Documentation & It's Management.

4. Jewellery Exports -Scope from India.

5. Export Import Finance Management with LC, ECGC & Venture Capital.

6. Shipping & Logistics in International Business with live links of Ports, ICDs, CHAs etc.

7. International Business Marketing Part 1: Finding Potential & Genuine Buyers for Exports and Suppliers for Imports.

8. International Business Marketing Part 2: Communication Skill to take repeated orders from Potential Buyers.

• • •

www.ingramcontent.com/pod-product-compliance
Lightning Source LLC
Chambersburg PA
CBHW040124150726

48005CB00015B/2355